Praying
for the
Peace of Jerusalem

PENNY VALENTINE

TAHILLA
Eastbourne

First published 2004

Published by Tahilla Communications
70 Milton Road, Eastbourne, East Sussex, BN21 1SS, UK.

ISBN 1 84291 187 2

Book design and production for the publisher by
Bookprint Creative Services, P.O. Box 827, BN21 3YJ, England.
Printed in Great Britain.

Contents

Foreword   5

Acknowledgements   7

Introduction   9

Teach Us to Pray – *Luke 11:1–13*   12

Pray for the Peace of Jerusalem – *Psalm 122*   14

Blessings and Curses – *Genesis 12:1–9*   16

Title Deeds – *Genesis 15*   18

Father of Many Nations – *Genesis 17:1–22*   20

Shechem – *Genesis 33:18 – 35:4*   22

Recognising Joseph – *Genesis 45:1–15*   24

Sacrifice to Molech – *Leviticus 18:19–30*   26

A People Dwelling Alone – *Numbers 23:7–24:9*   28

Power to Get Wealth – *Deuteronomy 8*   30

Whose Side Is God On? – *Joshua 5:13–6:16*   32

Ruth and Orpah – *Ruth 1:1–18*   34

The Sword and the Trowel – *Nehemiah 4*   36

Two Kinds of Words – *Psalm 12*   38

God Is in Control – *Psalm 33*   40

God Sees it All – *Psalm 94*   42

Mercy and Justice – *Psalm 101*   44

Joined with Israel – *Isaiah 14:1, 2*   46

One of Three – *Isaiah 19:16–25*   48

The Valley of Vision – *Isaiah 22:1–14*   50

In and Out of Office – *Isaiah 22:15–25*   52

A Call to the South – *Isaiah 43:1–7*   54

Save the Children – *Isaiah 49:14–26*   56

God's Ways Are not Ours – *Isaiah 55*   58

Repairer of the Breach – *Isaiah 58:9–12*   60

The Throne of the Lord – *Jeremiah 3:6–18*   62
A Fountain of Tears – *Jeremiah 8:15–9:1*   64
Drawn or Driven – *Jeremiah 16:14–21*   66
The Right of Inheritance – *Jeremiah 32*   68
Heart Transplant – *Ezekiel 11:14–21*   70
Standing in the Gap – *Ezekiel 22:23–31*   72
The Mountains of Israel – *Ezekiel 36:1–15*   74
For Your Name's Sake – *Ezekiel 36:16–38*   76
Understanding by the Books – *Daniel 9:1–22*   78
Going with God's People – *Zechariah 8:20–23*   80
Conditions of his Coming – *Matthew 23:29–24:14*   82
The Two Brothers – *Luke 15:11–32*   84
You Must Be Kidding! – *Romans 11:1–15*   86
Enemies For Our Sake – *Romans 11:16–36*   88
No Longer Strangers – *Ephesians 2:11–22*   90

List of Biblical Passages Used   93
Alphabetical List of Studies   94

Foreword

Penny Valentine has a special anointing from God for this book. As an intercessor herself, she lived and worked in the City of Jerusalem, helping intercessors worldwide to pray for the peace of that city.

In the book she reaches the heart of God and the practical concerns of everyday life in Israel.

There is only one thing in Scripture that the Lord says He does with all His heart. When Jerusalem is surrounded by danger, God speaks prophetically of His people Israel: '. . . the Lord, the God of Israel [says] concerning this city, [Jerusalem] . . . Behold, I will gather them out of all countries . . . and I will plant them in this land assuredly with my whole heart and with my whole soul' (Jeremiah 32:36–41 AV).

So God's heart for the re-gathering of Israel is here, but God is also a God of truth and justice, a God of compassion who hates the shedding of innocent blood. So Penny invites us through Scripture to receive God's heart concerning the media in Israel, issues of justice and the use of power, abortion, and the church in Israel today.

As Penny helps us to pray, we become partners with God in changing His world. Over twenty years ago I was working for an inter-governmental organisation committed to nudging the world to be a better place. After working for government ministers' meetings in health education and law, I concluded that prayer was the more effective tool of world change as we receive God's heart for His kingdom and pray as He taught us to do. That's why the Lord's Prayer comes first in this book.

As you read it seek His mind on the application of the Scriptures quoted. Each section can be used for personal devotions on a daily basis, or home groups could use it for fifteen minutes each week, spread over a year. In the peace of Jerusalem, the peace of the whole world will be found.

We value Rod and Penny Valentine's contribution to the ministry of Christian Friends of Israel in the UK, but this book goes beyond that role. It is not a statement of CFI's policy or calling, but the calling God puts on the heart of intercessors worldwide.

Geoffrey Smith
Deputy Director, CFI–UK

Acknowledgements

This book has been many years in the making, and many have helped along the way. Serving the Lord and Israel as volunteers in both Jerusalem and Africa for ten years would not have been possible without the practical support of some very special friends in Wales, England, South Africa and the USA, along with our home church fellowship in West Wales. Thank you all for your faithfulness over many years and your faith in Rod and me.

To my past and present colleagues in the ministry on three continents, I say thank you for your fellowship and all I have learned from working with you. In particular I am grateful to the Director and Trustees of CFI-UK for enabling me to write this book, and to my co-workers for many constructive comments. Geoffrey Smith, whose enthusiasm for this project has encouraged me greatly, deserves special thanks for all he has done in liaising with the publisher, and for writing the Foreword.

I would also like to thank my parents, Denis and Joan Cooper, with whom I shared my first experiences of Israel many years ago. They have stood with us all along the way.

Finally, a special thank you to my beloved husband Rod, with whom I am one in our joint calling to share God's heart for Israel with the heart of Christians everywhere, and to stand in love alongside His covenant people. He has been an invaluable critic and helped me persevere with the vision for this book – 'Just do it!'

Penny Valentine, December 2003

Introduction

How do we pray for the peace of Jerusalem? We know it is a command in Scripture, and we see from reports in our daily newspapers that it is very necessary. But most Christians haven't a clue how to understand such a complex and difficult situation, let alone what to pray for. There is only one source we can truly trust for guidance in how to pray, and that is God's word on the subject. This series of Bible studies is designed to help us understand some of the passages that throw light on God's purposes for Israel, and then make use of these Scriptures in focused prayer. That way, we will not pray according to our own understanding, but in co-operation with the Lord, to help fulfil His perfect will.

What's more, praying Scripture is powerful. Paul teaches us that the sword of the Spirit is the word of God (Ephesians 6:17). When we pray God's word, we are using the weapons He has given us to overcome the powers of darkness that would try to deny His word and thwart His purposes. We can pray in faith, confident of an answer because we are praying according to His blueprint (1 John 5:14).

Because it is important to view Scripture in context, each study gives a *passage* to be read and considered at the start, as well as some *guiding thoughts* about key verses. The *prayer points* that follow are designed to help us respond to truth with action, and build on understanding with intercession. A number of topics are covered, all greatly needing the prayers of the saints. It is my hope and prayer that the Holy Spirit will use these studies to help teach and inspire many to pray more effectively for the peace of Jerusalem and thus the salvation of the Jewish people and the return of the Messiah.

'Then the LORD answered me and said:
"Write the vision and make it plain on tablets,
that he may run who reads it"'
(Habakkuk 2:2).

TEACH US TO PRAY

> 'Now it came to pass, as He was praying in a certain place, when He ceased, that one of His disciples said to Him, "Lord, teach us to pray, as John also taught his disciples." So He said to them, "When you pray, say: . . ."' (Luke 11:1, 2).

 Passage for study and prayer: Luke 11:1–13

Like all Jewish rabbis, Jesus taught by example. In the Hebrew world of Jesus' time, teaching was not merely the transference of information and intellectual knowledge, but modelling the principles of God's word in every day life. Jewish students learned by being with their teachers constantly – watching, listening and asking questions that drew forth the wisdom and knowledge of their master. Luke perfectly illustrates this principle here, for Jesus' most profound teaching on prayer arose in a situation where His disciples had just watched and heard Him praying. He then gave them a model prayer to use, based on the words and principles of Scripture, like many other Jewish prayers found in the 'siddur' (Jewish prayer book) today.

We know the Lord's Prayer so well, we often don't think of praying it over specific situations. Yet it provides a wonderful framework for ensuring that we pray biblically and effectively. Firstly, it shows us who we pray to – our Father in heaven, the God of Israel who has become our Father through Jesus the Messiah, His Son. We long for His name to be sanctified (made holy, given glory) more and more, through our own actions and in the world at large. We deeply desire His kingdom, or Kingship, to be extended on earth in every situation, in the same way it is in heaven, where He rules supreme. We look to Him for provision of our needs, and for forgiveness and the grace to forgive others, for these things will lift up His name and extend His rule where we are. We trust Him to keep us from temptation and deliver us out of the hand of the evil one who works to thwart God's kingdom and steal His glory. What a prayer! No wonder it is powerful when prayed with real feeling and understanding. Use Jesus' model prayer to pray on behalf of Israel and the Jewish people:

Prayer Guide

Pray that the Father's name will be lifted up and sanctified as a result of all that happens in His land today, and through the lives of His chosen people.

Pray for God's perfect will to be accomplished through all that is currently going on in Israel and the Middle East, politically, diplomatically and in every area.

Pray earnestly for material provision for all Israel's needs. Especially remember new immigrants, single parents, large families, the unemployed, the disabled, and those trapped in circumstances of poverty.

Plead with God for mercy and forgiveness for His people in their many sins, and that they may be given much grace to forgive those who sin against them.

Pray for Israel in the many temptations she faces, that she may trust the Lord and choose to obey His word, and live according to the principles He has laid down.

Pray protection for Israel from all her enemies. Beseech God to deliver her from every plan of the evil one to destroy her and prevent her from fulfilling her destiny.

Go on persistently praying and pleading, as Jesus went on to teach in verses 5–13! *'For everyone who asks receives, and he who seeks finds, and to him who knocks it will be opened'* (v10).

PRAY FOR THE PEACE OF JERUSALEM

> *'Pray for the peace of Jerusalem: "May those who love you be secure. May there be peace within your walls and security within your citadels"'* (Psalm 122:6, 7 NIV).

 Passage for study and prayer: Psalm 122

What does it mean to pray for the peace of Jerusalem? The very name means 'city of peace' and yet it is the cause of greater conflict than any other city on earth. Reams have been written, endless hours spent pontificating on television, and political careers have even risen and fallen, all in the quest for the elusive 'Middle East Peace'. Yet the suffering on both sides only gets worse. Man's efforts will never bring peace. No wonder the Psalmist commands us to pray for it – but why and how?

Jerusalem is the house of the LORD, the place where He dwells and reveals Himself in a special way (v1). It has been carefully built according to His design (v3), to unify His people and bring them together to worship and praise Him according to His word, that they may be a testimony to Him (v4). It is the place where His rule and judgement are experienced (v5). Because Jerusalem is ordained by God to be the focal point of His presence and His people, (and eventually the place to which Messiah will return) we are actively to seek its prosperity and pray for its peace and security (vv8, 9).

No wonder the enemy tries every possible way to thwart God's purposes for this city! He has a counterfeit for every truth. To a Muslim, the House of Peace – Dar al Salaam – is every place where Islam rules, and thus until Jerusalem is completely ruled by Muslims, it is Dar al Hab, the House of War. In fact, true peace will not come to Jerusalem until it is again fully the House of the Lord, built together for His people both Jew and

Gentile, and ruled over by the Prince of Peace. That is what we are praying for when we pray for the peace of Jerusalem – the fulfilling of God's plan.

 Prayer Guide

Praise the Lord for all His purposes for Jerusalem – past, present and future! Proclaim His sovereignty over the city and all in it, and stand against every principality and power seeking to usurp His authority and thwart His purposes, especially all false religion, in the name of Jesus. Beseech God to build Jerusalem according to His special blueprint, to be His habitation amongst His covenant people. *'Jerusalem is built like a city that is closely compacted together'* (v3).

Pray earnestly that Jerusalem may remain under Jewish sovereignty. Pray too that many may go there to seek the God of Israel and worship Him in Spirit and truth. *'That is where the tribes go up, . . . to praise the name of the LORD . . .'* (v4). Pray for the revelation of Messiah to all the diverse inhabitants of Jerusalem, that they may be truly united in Him (see Ephesians 2:14). Especially uphold those believers living, worshipping and witnessing in Jerusalem in obedience to God's call.

Pray fervently for the Lord's special protection over Jerusalem, both physically and spiritually, and for the safety of all living there. *'For the sake of my brothers and friends, I will say, "Peace be within you"'* (v8). Pray too that many Christians may understand the importance of Jerusalem in God's plan and seek her good. *'For the sake of the house of the LORD our God, I will seek your prosperity'* (v9).

BLESSINGS AND CURSES

> *'I will make you a great nation; I will bless you and make your name great; and you shall be a blessing. I will bless those who bless you, and whoever curses you I will curse; and all peoples on earth will be blessed through you'* (Genesis 12:2, 3).

 Passage for study and prayer: Genesis 12:1–9

This promise of God to Abraham, applies also to the great nation that the Lord promised to make out of his descendants. It is one of the simplest and yet most profound of Biblical prophecies. It has already been abundantly fulfilled.

Who could deny the impact that the Jewish people have had upon history over the past millennia? God chose them to be the vehicle of His revelation to mankind. Without them, we would have no Bible and no Saviour – the Jewish Messiah, Jesus. Even on a more human level, the contribution of Jewish scientists, artists, musicians, and philosophers down through the centuries has been far out of proportion to their numbers. In our own day, Israel's hi-tech industries are at the forefront of research and development in such important areas as medicine and communications.

Yes, they have been a blessing, and still will be in the future, but they have also been a means of either blessing or cursing for others. Both the Bible and history show that those who bless Israel shall be blessed by God, and those that curse them (the Hebrew word 'qalal' meaning despise, revile, or treat with contempt) shall He curse, ('arar' meaning execrate, bitterly curse). All mankind faces the choice of what they will do with God's chosen people, and the Lord will judge them on their response.

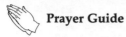 **Prayer Guide**

Thank God for the ways He has used Abraham's descendants to bless the world in the past, and especially for the blessings that you have received in your own life from the Jewish people. Pray for those in Israel who are engaged in research in the fields of medicine, information technology, agriculture etc, that their work may be prospered and inspired by God Himself. '. . . *I will bless you; I and will make your name great; and you will be a blessing'* (v2).

Pray for Israel as a nation to fulfil her divine calling to be a channel of blessing to all the families of the earth in the coming days in preparation for the return of the Messiah. Stand against the attempts by the enemy to rob her of this calling by every means. 'And God said to Balaam, ". . . *you shall not curse the people, for they are blessed"'* (Numbers 22:12 NIV).

Diligently pray for your own family, church and nation to take a position of blessing rather than cursing towards Israel and the Jewish people. *'For the nation and kingdom which will not serve you shall perish, and those nations shall be utterly ruined'* (Isaiah 60:12).

TITLE DEEDS

> *'Then He said to him [Abram], "I am the LORD, who brought*
> *you out of Ur of the Chaldeans, to give you this land to inherit*
> *it." And he said, "Lord GOD, how shall I know that I will*
> *inherit it?"'* (Genesis 15:7, 8).

 Passage for study and prayer: Genesis 15

God had previously promised to give the land of Canaan to
Abram as his inheritance (Genesis 12:7; 13:15); but this time,
Abram asked for some kind of proof. It is all very well to
receive a promise, but how could he know that it would actually happen? The Lord's answer was very tangible. He 'cut a
covenant' with Abram, according to the ancient rituals of the
time, where animals would be cut in half and the two parties
to a legal agreement would pass between the two halves in a
figure of eight, symbolising their acceptance of its terms and
conditions. From that time the covenant would be legal and
binding on both parties.

Abram follows the Lord's instructions and gets everything
ready for the ritual, but while he waits, a deep and terrible
sleep falls upon him. God speaks further to him of his future
descendants and the land – the two major elements of His
promise and this covenant. Then, in the visible form of a fire-
pot with a blazing flame, the Lord Himself passes between the
sacrificial pieces, thus legally 'signing' this covenant deed. The
interesting thing is, that Abram himself does not do so. This is
a one-sided covenant. Unlike the later covenant made with
Israel through Moses, there are no conditions. All the commitment is on the Lord's side, and Abram's part is simply to
believe. The gift of the land of Canaan to Abram's descendants
is purely one of grace.

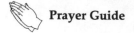 **Prayer Guide**

Praise God for his commitment to His people, and His wonderful plans for them throughout history! Pray diligently for the Jewish people to have faith like Abram, believing in God and His Word, and pleasing Him by their faithfulness: *'And he believed in the* LORD, *and He accounted it to him for righteousness'* (v6).

Give thanks for the miracle that once again Israel is a nation in its own land, proving the faithfulness of the LORD to His word! Declare in prayer that it belongs to the Jewish people as their inheritance, by covenant gift of God: *'On the same day the* LORD *made a covenant with Abram, saying: "To your descendants I have given this land, from the river of Egypt to the great river, the River Euphrates —"'* (v18). May He bring them into their full inheritance in His perfect time and way.

Pray earnestly for all of Abraham's descendants – Jewish, Muslim and Christian – who share the land today. Pray that they may dwell together in peace according to God's perfect purpose for all of them, under the leadership of His covenant people.

FATHER OF MANY NATIONS

> *'No longer shall your name be called Abram, but your name shall be Abraham; for I have made you a father of many nations'* (Genesis 17:5).

 Passage for study and prayer: Genesis 17:1–22

The Tomb of the Patriarchs in Hebron, where Abraham and Sarah are buried along with Isaac and Jacob, is one of the flash points of the Arab-Israeli conflict. This is not surprising – part of it is a synagogue where Jews worship the God of Israel, and part is a mosque for Arab worshippers of Allah, the Muslim deity. Abraham is considered the father of both the Jewish and Arab nations, through his sons Isaac and Ishmael. Both peoples carry the sign of the covenant, circumcision, in their flesh, and claim the covenant as theirs – but the Bible makes it very clear that as far as God is concerned, Isaac is the only legal heir. Isaac's descendants alone – through his own younger son Jacob, (not Esau, who is also an ancestor of the Arab people) – would belong to God in a special way and in turn the land of Canaan would belong to them.

Abraham liked this idea as little as some of his descendants have since! His first response to the news that Sarah would miraculously bear him a son in their old age, was simple unbelief. He tried to persuade God that his beloved son Ishmael, born of his slave girl Hagar in an attempt to provide himself an heir, would do just as well – but God said 'No'. Whilst He would also bless Ishmael, give him an inheritance of land in the Middle East and make him a great nation, the covenant would be established with Isaac. God was not being unfair. One of the nations born of Abraham's seed had to be set apart in a special way to be God's instrument. Through Isaac's family

20

He would reveal His character and eventually fulfil His plan, to bring *all* nations into covenant relationship with Himself. The sons of Ishmael would then be able to share in the covenant through faith in Messiah Jesus, and be reconciled to their brethren. Right now the Arabs, in bondage to a counterfeit religion, and the Jews, still unredeemed as a people, are each God's instrument of judgement for the other – but the day will come when they will be a witness together of His grace.

 Prayer Guide

Praise God for His *everlasting* covenant with the Jewish people, and pray that all His perfect purposes for the land and nation of Israel will be fulfilled, for the blessing of the nations. *'Also I give to you and your descendants after you the land in which you are a stranger, all the land of Canaan, as an everlasting possession; and I will be their God'* (v8).

Pray earnestly and with love for all Arab people to be set free from the bondage of Islam and come into the fulfilment of God's blessing and promise for them. *'And Abraham said to God, "Oh, that Ishmael might live before You!"'* (v18).

Stand in prayer for Hebron, where God spoke these words to Abraham and gave the promise of the land to Isaac's seed. It is a place of great spiritual as well as physical conflict and challenge to the truth of God's word. *'But My covenant I will establish with Isaac, whom Sarah shall bear to you at this set time next year'* (v21).

SHECHEM

'Then Jacob came safely to the city of Shechem, . . . And he bought the parcel of land, where he had pitched his tent, from the children of Hamor, Shechem's father, for one hundred pieces of money. Then he erected an altar there and called it El Elohe Israel [i.e. God, the God of Israel]' (Genesis 33:18–20).

 Passage for study and prayer: Genesis 33:18–35:4

Spiritually, Shechem (New Testament Samaria) is a gateway to Israel's inheritance and a witness to the God of Israel. Abraham built an altar there on arrival in Canaan (Genesis 12:6, 13:4). It was also Jacob's first stop after his exile in Padan Aram. He purchased land from the local ruler where he also built an altar dedicated to the God of Israel. Relations were friendly, but sadly, things went wrong. The awful story of Dinah and the prince of Shechem, with wickedness and treachery causing a breach between two peoples, began a bloody saga that can be followed throughout the Bible. Many times Shechem features as the scene of division, violence, betrayal and bloodshed. At the same time, it is a place where God repeatedly called His people to choose between Himself and idols, and where they renewed their covenant with Him.

It seems that because of its significance as a gateway and place of worship, there has always been great spiritual warfare connected with Shechem. The enemy will do all he can to pervert God's purposes. He has exploited Israel's weaknesses, fostered idolatry and division, built strongholds of evil and hatred on shed blood that has defiled the land. Today, biblical Shechem is called Nablus. It is now a large Arab town, a hotbed of terrorism directed against Israel and a place of great suffering for both Jews and Arabs. Joseph's tomb in Nablus, with its ancient synagogue and 'yeshiva' (religious centre), is a focus of the spiritual battle. During the Palestinian uprising of 2000, the Jews were attacked and driven out and it was immediately made into a mosque. Although the site was later reclaimed, Jewish worship continues only under armed guard.

 Prayer Guide

Give thanks that from the earliest times this area has been dedicated to the God of Israel, the one true God. Proclaim His sovereignty over Shechem/Nablus, and stand against all false gods that seek to usurp His authority. *'O LORD our God, masters besides you have had dominion over us: but by you only we make mention of your name'* (Isaiah 26:13).

Implore the Lord in His mercy to forgive the sins of His people both past and present, especially the shedding of innocent blood in this place, on the basis of the atonement provided through the blood of Jesus. *'Rejoice, O Gentiles, with His people; for He will avenge the blood of His servants, and render vengeance to His adversaries; He will provide atonement for His land and His people'* (Deuteronomy 32:43).

Pray for those who live in Nablus and the surrounding communities and villages, both Jewish and Arab, to be set free from the cycle of revenge and hatred. Pray for a desire for peace to rise in their hearts and for the Holy Spirit to bring true reconciliation. *'When a man's ways please the LORD, He makes even his enemies to be at peace with him'* (Proverbs 16:7).

RECOGNISING JOSEPH

> 'Then Joseph could not restrain himself before all those who stood by him, and he cried out, "Make everyone go out from me!" So no one stood with him while Joseph made himself known to his brothers' (Genesis 45:1).

 Passage for study and prayer: Genesis 45:1–15

What made Joseph unable to restrain himself any longer from revealing himself to his brothers? He had been dealing with them for some time, continuing to hide his identity and true relationship whilst he tested them to see if they had changed over the years since they had so harshly rejected him and sold him into slavery. But suddenly the moment came when he was so overcome with emotion, with love and longing to be part of the family again, that he just had to tell them who he was. What made the difference?

The answer lies in the preceding chapter. Benjamin was Joseph's full blood brother, the only one to share the same father *and* mother. He was especially close to Joseph's heart. Joseph had made sure that Benjamin would become as he had been, unjustly made a slave in a foreign land. And here was Judah, who had been one of the prime movers in his own sale into slavery, offering to take Benjamin's place and bear his punishment, to spare a repeat of his father's anguish at losing yet another son. This act of loving sacrifice was what brought Joseph to the point where he couldn't wait a minute longer. He dismissed all others from the room. Alone with his brothers for that sacred moment, he no longer spoke in a foreign tongue but in their own language, and they finally saw beneath the alien garb and recognised him for who he truly was.

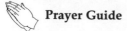 **Prayer Guide**

Praise the Lord that the time is coming when the brethren of Jesus 'according to the flesh' will see Him as He is, and understand God's purposes in their previous rejection of Him. *'But now, do not therefore be grieved or angry with your-selves because you sold me here; for God sent me before you to preserve life'* (v5).

Pray fervently that the Gentile covering that currently keeps so many Jews from recognising Jesus as their Messiah will be stripped away, and they will enter into true fellowship with Him through His word. *'Moreover he kissed all his brothers and wept over them, and after that his brothers talked with him'* (v15).

Pray for Christians to be so moved with love and compassion for the people of Israel, Jesus' 'full brothers', that they will be willing to sacrificially identify with them no matter what it costs, and so hasten the day when Messiah will reveal Himself. *'. . .please let your servant remain instead of the lad as a slave to my lord, . . .'* (Genesis 44:33).

SACRIFICE TO MOLECH

> *'And you shall not let any of your descendants pass through the fire to Molech, nor shall you profane the name of your God: I am the LORD'* (Leviticus 18:21).

 Passage for study and prayer: Leviticus 18:19–30

Molech (or Milcam), was the god of the Ammonites. His worship involved human sacrifice, usually of children. 'Its image was a hollow brazen figure, with the head of an ox, and outstretched human arms. It was heated red hot by a fire from within, and the little ones placed in its arms to be slowly burned, while to prevent the parents from hearing the dying cries, the sacrificing priests beat drums' (Thayer's Greek Definitions). Today, Molech is a forgotten god, but in Israel as elsewhere, the sacrifice of children continues on a huge scale through the accepted practice of abortion. In spite of the generally high Jewish regard for the sanctity of life, Israel has a liberal abortion policy. Female soldiers are routinely provided two free abortions during their two-year national service, whilst many Russian immigrants have a history of multiple pregnancy terminations. Abortion occurs throughout all of Israel's diverse society, among rich and poor, Jew and Arab, religious and secular.

Leviticus 18 places child sacrifice firmly in the context of aberrant sexual behaviour. To sacrifice your offspring is as contrary to the true purpose of sexual union between man and woman as is adultery, homosexuality or bestiality. All are a profound offence to the Creator who made mankind in His image, and profane His name. Abortion is often the result of breaking God's laws of sexual purity and fidelity. Also, we find that such behaviour deeply defiles those who engage in it, and also their communities. Even the land itself is depicted as violently vomiting out its inhabitants as God brings judgement for such iniquity. Indeed, that is why he removed Israel's predecessors from the land, and gave it to them! He expects His own people to have higher standards than others, to reflect His own name and nature. Abortion deeply traumatises the parents, as those involved in post-abortion counselling know only too well. What's more, the effect is felt within the whole society, as soaring levels of domestic violence and other family problems in Israel prove.

 Prayer Guide

Plead with God to convict Israeli society of the sin of sacrificing their unborn children to the idols of selfishness, pride, fear or unbelief. *'Do not defile yourselves with any of these things; for by all these the nations are defiled, which I am casting out before you'* (v24). Pray for those contemplating abortion to have a change of heart. Pray the same for doctors, social workers and legislators who support abortion.

Give thanks for the pro-life work in Israel, and pray earnestly for much fruit from the outreaches via literature, advertisements and help lines from several centres around the country. Beseech God to provide all the necessary finances, protect and anoint all personnel, and bring new life and hope to many through this vital service.

Pray for the healing of the land from the defilement of the shedding of innocent blood, and for Israel to truly reflect the nature and character of her God, as He intended. *'You ... shall not commit any of these abominations, either any of your own nation or any stranger who dwells among you'* (v26). Pray also for the Palestinians. They not only practise abortion, but also permit their sons and daughters to be sacrificed as suicide 'martyrs' on the altar of nationalism and political expediency.

A PEOPLE DWELLING ALONE

> *'How shall I curse whom God has not cursed? And how shall I denounce whom the LORD has not denounced? For from the top of the rocks I see him, and from the hills I behold him; There! A people dwelling alone, not reckoning itself among the nations'* (Numbers 23:8, 9).

 Passage for study and prayer: Numbers 23:7–24:9

Even though Israel today longs to be reckoned among the nations and treated just like any other country, instead of having to fight for her right to exist, it has been her prophetic destiny since the time of Moses to be a people dwelling alone. As a people whom God has called and blessed for His own prophetic purposes in the world, she has always been feared and misunderstood by her neighbours, who have sought just as Balak king of Moab did, to find ways to curse and destroy her. (Numbers 23:3–6).

However, the wonderful lesson of the story of Balaam, the prophet hired by Balak, is that it is impossible for man to curse the people whom God has blessed! All Balak's repeated efforts simply resulted in more blessings being pronounced, whilst the cost to him increased each time. This story recorded in Numbers 22–24 is startlingly relevant to today's situation, where despite the sinfulness and failings of Israel, her enemies' attempts to overcome her simply result in more suffering and despair for themselves. Whilst God will use them to chastise her according to His will, He will also use Israel as a standard by which to judge them and to reveal His sovereign power over the nations.

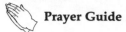 **Prayer Guide**

Praise the Lord that His sovereign choice of Israel cannot be denied and will result in blessing for the nation in God's purposes. *'God is not a man, that He should lie, nor a son of man, that He should repent. Has He said, and will He not do? . . . Behold, I have received a command to bless; He has blessed, and I cannot reverse it'* (23:19, 20).

Proclaim over all those nations and peoples who would seek to do Israel harm, *'For there is no sorcery against Jacob, nor any divination against Israel. It now must be said of Jacob and of Israel, "Oh, what God has done!"'* (23:23). Cry out for God's glory to be revealed to the nations through Israel in the times ahead.

Pray fervently for the nations of the world, and especially Israel's neighbours, to choose blessing not cursing in their response to Israel at this time – *'Blessed is he who blesses you, and cursed is he who curses you'* (24:9b). Stand against the anti-Semitism, disguised as anti-Zionism, which is again on the rise in Europe and other Western countries, and pray for those in the Jewish and Christian communities who are seeking to combat it.

POWER TO GET WEALTH

> *'And you shall remember the L*ORD *your God, for it is He who gives you power to get wealth, that He may establish His covenant which He swore to your fathers, as it is this day'* (Deuteronomy 8:18).

 Passage for study and prayer: Deuteronomy 8

This passage contains God's economic policy for His people. It all begins with obedience to His commandments or instructions (vv1, 2). The children of Israel had to learn in the wilderness that the real source of their physical life and provision was God Himself, and His word (vv3, 4). Secondly, God uses the matter of practical needs as an instrument of correction, to chasten His children where necessary and bring them back to His ways (v5). Thirdly, His plan and desire is to bless and prosper them physically as well as spiritually. Hence He gives them a good land, wherein they will have everything they need, not only to survive but to enjoy (vv6–9).

However, there is a stern warning for Israel in verses 10–17. The human heart so easily slips into ingratitude and carelessness, selfishness and idolatry. If we do not remember the source of our wealth, prosperity can quickly lead to pride. We take the credit for our own success and trust in our own efforts, rather than blessing God for His goodness and giving Him the glory. The thing is, there is an underlying purpose behind material blessing of God. It is so that He may establish His covenant that He promised to His people. He wants to fulfil His purposes for Israel as a nation, but that is only possible when they obey Him. It is only a step from careless arrogance, to outright worship of gods other than the Lord Himself. And that is the way of death and destruction.

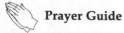 **Prayer Guide**

Thank God for the way He has prospered Israel in her short half century as a reborn nation, for the sake of His covenant. Pray that her people will not take His blessings for granted, nor take the credit for success, but be thankful. *'When you have eaten and are full, then you shall bless the LORD your God for the good land which He has given you . . . lest . . . your heart is lifted up, and you forget the LORD your God . . . then you say in your heart, "My power and the might of my hand have gained me this wealth"'* (vv10, 12, 14, 17).

Pray for real change and an end to corruption and injustice wherever it is found. In recent years, Israel's economy has suffered severely as a result of Palestinian Arab terrorism and ongoing violence. Pray for the nation to be convicted by this economic chastening, of her failure to live up to God's standards of righteousness. *'You should know in your heart that as a man chastens his son, so the LORD your God chastens you. Therefore you shall keep the commandments of the LORD your God, to walk in His ways and to fear Him'* (vv5, 6).

Pray that in these difficult times the people of Israel may cry out to their God as their provider, and turn afresh to His word. *'So He humbled you, allowed you to hunger, and fed you with manna . . . that He might make you know that man shall not live by bread alone; but man lives by every word that proceeds from the mouth of the LORD'* (v3). Beseech the Lord in His mercy to give His people power to prosper economically. May He use their difficulties for their ultimate blessing: *'. . . that He might humble you and that He might test you, to do you good in the end –'* (v16).

WHOSE SIDE IS GOD ON?

> 'Now when Joshua was near Jericho, he looked up and saw a man standing in front of him with a drawn sword in his hand. Joshua went up to him and asked, "Are you for us or for our enemies?" "Neither," he replied, "but as commander of the army of the LORD I have now come"' (Joshua 5:13, 14 NIV).

 Passage for study and prayer: Joshua 5:13–6:16

These days, as the whole world takes sides in the ongoing Arab-Israeli conflict, believers in Jesus need to remember Joshua's experience, as he was about to lead the people of Israel into the Promised Land. The Man he saw was the Commander of the armies of Yahweh, and He did not fight on either side against the other. Instead, He had his own agenda, to command the will and purpose of God in the coming battle. Likewise today, the Lord does not take sides in a human sense, and neither must we. It is all too easy to let our flesh rise up and produce ungodly motives, so that we find ourselves praying for Israel and the Middle East out of a wrong spirit or from a limited human perspective. Those kinds of prayers do not get very far.

Instead, like Joshua, we need to worship (v14), listen for God's word (v14), and obey the call to holiness (v15). It was only after this personal encounter with his Commander, this obedience and consecration, that Joshua was given detailed instructions on how to fight God's way for Jericho. His battle became obedience to God, rather than overcoming his adversaries. Face to face with the Man, he received the anointing to be the Lord's instrument and part of His army. What a lesson this is for us. To be effective intercessors, we must be in close fellowship with Him, knowing His word, seeking His will, and living in a way that reflects His character. Then we pray with His heart and Spirit. What a challenge, but what a blessing!

 Prayer Guide

Praise God that this conflict is above all a spiritual one, led by the Lord Himself, with whom you have a personal relationship! Seek Him for His heart for all peoples involved, so you may pray according to His agenda and with His love in the days ahead. *'What does my Lord say to His servant?'* (v14).

Pray for the peoples on both sides of this war, who have suffered much and are filled with a growing anger and despair. Stand against strongholds of hatred and revenge, and pray for God to grant grace to forgive. *'Hatred stirs up strife, but love covers all sins'* (Proverbs 10:12).

Pray fervently that all the suffering and evil experienced by both Israelis and Palestinians will lead many to faith in the Prince of Peace. God's will is definitely and primarily for the spiritual salvation of Israel and all the peoples of the Middle East. *'A man will be as a hiding place from the wind, and a cover from the tempest, as rivers of water in a dry place, as the shadow of a great rock in a weary land'* (Isaiah 32:2).

RUTH AND ORPAH

> 'Then they lifted up their voices and wept again; and Orpah kissed her mother-in-law, but Ruth clung to her. And she said, "Look, your sister-in-law has gone back to her people and to her gods; return after your sister-in-law"' (Ruth 1:14, 15).

 Passage for study and prayer: Ruth 1:1–18

The Moabite women Ruth and Orpah reacted very differently to the same situation. They had married Jewish brothers, who both died within ten years. They were living with their widowed mother-in-law when she decided to return to the land of Israel, having heard that the famine that originally drove the family into Moab was over. Both travelled with her for a while on the road, until Naomi begged them to return to their mothers' homes, where they would have more chance of finding another husband and thus some future security. Both wept, both insisted they would return with her to her people, but when she reminded them that she could not assure their future, Orpah wavered. Her love for Naomi was not strong enough to draw her away from her own family and culture into an uncertain future, so she kissed her goodbye and turned back. Ruth on the other hand, clung to Naomi and would not let her go. Her passionate words of love and commitment are amongst the best known in the Scriptures. She loves enough to be determined to stay by Naomi's side, to be with her through thick and thin, to identify fully with her people and her God.

Gentile Christians today face the choice, like Ruth and Orpah, of whether to cling to the Jewish people in love, no matter what it costs, or walk away from them. The rest of Ruth's story shows that there was blessing beyond imagining for her in the choice she made. What's more, through her love and obedience she offered new life and hope not only to Naomi but the entire people of Israel and even of the world, in becoming the great-grandmother of King David and an ancestor of the Messiah.

 Prayer Guide

Stand in the gap for the Church today as it has to choose whether to stand alongside Israel in love and commitment, in the face of growing opposition, or not. Pray for denominations, congregations and individual Christians to be like Ruth rather than Orpah: *'. . . For wherever you go, I will go; and wherever you lodge, I will lodge; your people shall be my people, and your God, my God'* (v16).

Give thanks for those Gentiles who are already standing with the Jewish people, in Israel and elsewhere, and intercede for them. Pray for grace, wisdom and courage for them, and for perseverance in the face of spiritual opposition and difficult circumstances. *'Where you die, I will die, and there will I be buried. The LORD do so to me, and more also, if anything but death parts you and me'* (v17).

Pray for the building of relationships of love and trust between the Jewish and Christian communities in Israel and in the nations, especially your own nation, and ask God to use them for great blessing to both groups.

THE SWORD AND THE TROWEL

> *'Those who built on the wall, and those who carried burdens, loaded themselves so that with one hand they worked at construction, and with the other held a weapon. Every one of the builders had his sword girded at his side as he built . . .'* (Nehemiah 4:17, 18).

 Passage for study and prayer: Nehemiah 4

Uniquely among the nations, Israel celebrates her Independence Day in tandem with Remembrance Day, to honour the many thousands who have fallen in defence of the nation since the state was founded. (By her 55th birthday, the count was 21,540 soldiers and some three thousand civilian terrorist victims.) For 24 hours before the festivities marking the miracle of the rebirth of the Jewish nation begin, all Jews solemnly remember the high human cost of their freedom. Indeed, ever since Jews started returning to Zion in larger numbers in the 1880s, the pattern has been the same. The early pioneers worked to tame the land and build their future with their tools in one hand, and a weapon of defence against marauding Arab bandits in the other.

In fact, nothing has changed since Nehemiah's time! Israel's enemies are always aroused to utter fury by her efforts to rebuild her nation and reclaim her heritage. Today, they use the same tactics – mockery, intimidation, lies and slander and conspiracy to violence. There is clearly an underlying spiritual dimension to this conflict, which does not want to see God's purposes for Jerusalem and His people Israel fulfilled. Nehemiah refused to be intimidated and organised a co-operative defence plan, which involved some being set aside to guard others as they worked to rebuild the wall. Even those working carried their weapons in case they needed to defend themselves, as many in Israel do today. Above all, Nehemiah called upon God to act on behalf of His people to save them from the schemes of their enemies. He did. The plot was uncovered, the people were encouraged and the wall was built. God will do the same today, in answer to our fervent prayer.

 Prayer Guide

Beseech the Lord to expose and foil the plots of His enemies, aimed at driving His people out of their land. '. . . *God had brought their plot to nothing . . .'* (v15). Stand against the lying, deceiving spirit behind the anti-Israel propaganda filling our news media and pray that truth will prevail. *'Hear, O our God, for we are despised; turn their reproach on their own heads, and give them as plunder to a land of captivity! Do not cover their iniquity, . . .'* (vv4, 5).

Pray for encouragement, strength and perseverance for the Israeli people in the face of the constant physical and spiritual opposition that wears them down and tempts them to despair. *'Then Judah said, "The strength of the labourers is failing, and there is so much rubbish that we are not able to build the wall"'* (v10).

Give thanks for the vigilance of the various branches of the Israel Defence Forces who are Israel's 'sword' of protection against her enemies. Pray for them all for protection, wisdom, grace, courage and compassion; officers, young conscripts, and the reservists who leave jobs and family to do army duty. '. . . *Do not be afraid of them. Remember the Lord, great and awesome, and fight for your brethren, your sons, your daughters, your wives, and your houses'* (v14).

TWO KINDS OF WORDS

> 'Help, LORD, for the godly man ceases! For the faithful disappear from among the sons of men. They speak idly everyone with his neighbour; with flattering lips and a double heart they speak' (Psalm 12:1, 2).

 Passage for study and prayer: Psalm 12

How many of us who love Israel have felt just like David did when he wrote this Psalm? We read the newspapers or listen to the radio or television, and cringe when we hear misrepresentations, bias and even what we know to be downright lies spoken as truth. Sound bites, which are usually simplistic and incomplete, give false impressions and shape the views and even actions of millions who do not know the full story. Even in our own minds confusion can grow, as we wonder if what we believe or understand is really the truth or just propaganda from the other side – can the media and all the 'experts' really be wrong, and me, right?

David hits the nail right on the head when he cries out to God for help! He recognises that deception is subtle and that words are powerful weapons, for good or evil. When what is vile is lifted up in the public mind, it gives the wicked free rein. But the Lord Himself, whose own words are the only pure truth we can depend on, will act on behalf of those who suffer at their hands. Only the Lord can cut off the power of lies. He will not only keep His own word, but He will arise to help those who are oppressed and insecure because of the lying words of others. And His pure word, free of all selfish motives or agendas, is the only sure standard by which we can judge the words and actions of others, and on which we can base our own views and opinions.

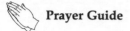 **Prayer Guide**

Proclaim the truth that God Himself is Lord over all those who speak false and evil words and ask Him to cut off their influence. *'May the LORD cut off all flattering lips, and the tongue that speaks proud things, who have said, "With our tongue we will prevail; our lips are our own; who is Lord over us?"'* (vv3, 4).

Claim God's promise for all who are oppressed and needy in Israel at this time. Israelis today are very worn down by the constant barrage of negative words which are spoken against them in the world's media, which make the hardships of their situation even harder to bear. *'Because of the oppression of the weak and the groaning of the needy, I will now arise', says the LORD. 'I will protect them from those who malign them'* (v5 NIV).

Pray for all those who are seeking to make the biblical and historical truths about Israel known in today's hostile climate, and ask God to use them powerfully to counteract lies and propaganda, which give opportunity to the evil one. *'The wicked prowl on every side, when vileness is exalted among the sons of men'* (v8).

GOD IS IN CONTROL

> 'The LORD brings the counsel of the nations to nothing; He makes the plans of the peoples of no effect. The counsel of the LORD stands forever, the plans of His heart to all generations' (Psalm 33:10, 11).

 Passage for study and prayer: Psalm 33

In today's seemingly crazy and unjust world, how inexpressibly comforting it is to reflect on the truth that God is in control! What a cause for rejoicing (vv1–3)! In spite of all appearances, the earth is full of His goodness. He is all that the world is not. In a world where lies and deception abound, His word is truth; in the midst of injustice and false accusations, his works are faithful and righteous (vv4, 5). The Psalmist reminds us that He made it all – the world, and all its inhabitants (vv6–9). He is sovereign over all of His creation, from the stars in the heavens to the heart of every individual, which He knows and judges according to their works (vv13–15).

He is also Lord of history. He has a plan for mankind that cannot be thwarted by the efforts of men. Neither their wisdom nor their strength can save them, in human terms, and their trust in their own strength is in vain (vv16, 17). God's blueprint will happen, as it has been ordained from the beginning of time. The nation of Israel is at the heart of His plan for His world, and He will continue to reduce to zero, all the pontificating proposals of the nations regarding her and her Arab neighbours. Peace Plans, Road Maps, United Nations Resolutions – none will succeed unless they specifically further the plans of God's heart for His beloved people. And in the midst of turmoil and suffering, His power and mercy is the source of their hope (vv18–22). Hallelujah!

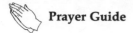 **Prayer Guide**

Pray through this psalm on behalf of Israel. Worship God for His wonderful unchanging character, His love, mercy, righteousness and power, at work even in the midst of the tragic situation in the Middle East. *'For the word of the LORD is right, and all His work is done in truth. He loves righteousness and justice; the earth is full of the goodness of the LORD'* (vv4, 5).

Proclaim over all the plans of the nations seeking to further their own agendas in the Middle East, that *'The LORD brings the counsel of the nations to nothing; He makes the plans of the peoples of no effect'* (v10). Rejoice that God's purposes are eternal and unchanging and cannot be destroyed or deflected. *'The counsel of the LORD stands forever, the plans of His heart to all generations'* (v11).

Give thanks for God's blessing on Israel, His chosen people, and all joined to them through faith in Jesus. *'Blessed is the nation whose God is the LORD, the people He has chosen as His own inheritance'* (v12). Pray that in the midst of the suffering, tensions and difficulties they experience, they may look to Him for mercy, protection and hope. *'Let Your mercy, O LORD, be upon us, just as we hope in You'* (v22).

GOD SEES IT ALL

> *'They pour out arrogant words; all the evildoers are full of boasting. They crush your people, O LORD; they oppress your inheritance. They slay the widow and the alien; they murder the fatherless. They say, "The LORD does not see; the God of Jacob pays no heed"'* (Psalm 94:4–7 NIV).

 Passage for study and prayer: Psalm 94

These verses read like Israeli newspapers. They could be describing the horrific carnage at the scene of a suicide bombing, as special religious volunteers scrape up the fragments of victims for proper burial. Or the terror attack with gun or bomb against soft targets – women, children and foreign workers – all going about their daily lives before suddenly entering eternity. Those responsible for the atrocities are jubilant when they succeed, they boast as they claim responsibility, completely disregarding the fact that Israel's God will hold them accountable for what they do.

Of course such attacks have gone on throughout the history of the Jewish people. No wonder they often cry to God with the question, 'How long will the wicked triumph?' The truth is, the Lord sees it all. He is the Creator, and He cannot be fooled or misled. The One who made the very faculties of sight and hearing, doesn't miss a single thing. He is the Judge of the earth, who disciplines nations, including Israel herself, in order to teach and correct them. He will deal with the wicked in His own time, and until then, He sustains His people in the midst of their suffering. He will never abandon or forsake them. He gives them rest in the midst of turmoil, comfort in anxiety, assurance of His help to keep them from falling, delight in His love to keep them going. Those with a real relationship to the Lord can go on in faith and trust no matter what, and leave the question of vengeance to Him.

 Prayer Guide

Call on the Lord to rise up and deal with those who defy Him in oppressing His people: *'O LORD, the God who avenges, O God who avenges, shine forth. Rise up, O Judge of the earth; pay back to the proud what they deserve'* (vv1, 2). Give thanks that the Lord sees men's hearts and knows their motives, and that all His dealings are to teach and bring to repentance: *'Does he who disciplines nations not punish? Does he who teaches man lack knowledge? The LORD knows the thoughts of man; he knows that they are futile'* (vv10, 11).

Pray earnestly that this psalm might become the experience of the Israeli people, as you pray through each verse on their behalf. Cry out that they may come into real relationship with their God. *'Who will take a stand for me against evildoers? Unless the LORD had given me help, I would soon have dwelt in the silence of death'* (vv16b, 17).

Remember especially the victims of terror attacks and their families, who are struggling to cope with the after-effects of their experiences. *'When I said, "My foot is slipping," your love, O LORD, supported me. When anxiety was great within me, your consolation brought joy to my soul'* (vv18, 19).

Pray for encouragement for all those who are facing despair and depression in the face of unrelenting hatred, for faith and hope to rise in their hearts: *'But the LORD has become my fortress, and my God the rock in whom I take refuge'* (v22).

MERCY AND JUSTICE

> *'I will sing of mercy and justice; to You, O LORD, I will sing praises'* (Psalm 101:1).

 Passage for study and prayer: Psalm 101

This Psalm was written by David, King of Israel, at a time when he was very conscious of his responsibility to lead his people – probably at the outset of his reign. It is a hymn of praise to God, and also a promise to honour Him faithfully in his life and leadership – a wonderful example for us to follow in our own service to the Lord! Mercy (the Hebrew 'chesed', meaning lovingkindness, compassion, steadfast love), and justice or righteous judgement ('mishpat' in Hebrew) are two characteristics that David has abundantly experienced in God's dealings with him over past years. Now, he resolves that as king, they will shape his own response to the challenges that lie ahead.

David, as a finite human being, didn't always succeed in ruling according to these principles, but he tried, and even in his failures, he remained open to the Lord. How much Israel needs leaders like this today, in every sphere of her public life! To lead God's people, whose very existence is to be a witness to Him and His faithfulness, is a huge challenge and an awesome responsibility. How much those in leadership need to follow David's example and resolve in their hearts to depend on God and determine to do right.

 **Prayer Guide**

Pray for Israel's leaders to be men of integrity who desire and determine to govern with wisdom and righteousness. *'I will behave wisely in a perfect way . . .'* (v2). May God give them grace to shun corruption and wickedness in all its forms and be strengthened to resist temptation. *'I will set nothing wicked before my eyes; I hate the work of those who fall away; it shall not cling to me. A perverse heart shall depart from me; I will not know wickedness'* (vv3, 4). Particularly remember the Prime Minister and Cabinet Ministers in their great responsibilities.

Pray for the Lord to raise up godly men and women to serve in the Knesset (Parliament), in local government in the various towns and cities and in leadership of the armed forces, police, unions and other public bodies. Pray for honesty and public spirit to replace political opportunism, self-seeking and corruption and for those of integrity to be prospered. *'The one who has a haughty look and a proud heart, him I will not endure. My eyes shall be on the faithful of the land, that they may dwell with me; he who walks in a perfect way, he shall serve me'* (vv5b, 6).

Pray especially for the judicial system in Israel, the Middle East's only democracy. Uphold the Attorney General, members of the Supreme Court and all involved in dispensing justice within the nation, that they may be given wisdom and integrity in all situations. *'He who works deceit shall not dwell within my house; he who tells lies shall not continue in my presence. Early I will destroy all the wicked of the land, that I may cut off all the evildoers from the city of the LORD'* (vv7, 8).

JOINED WITH ISRAEL

> *'For the LORD will have mercy on Jacob, and will still choose Israel, and settle them in their own land. The strangers will be joined with them, and they will cling to the house of Jacob. Then people will take them and bring them to their place, and the house of Israel will possess them for servants and maids in the land of the Lord; . . .'* (Isaiah 14:1, 2).

 Passage for study and prayer: Isaiah 14:1, 2

It is by God's compassion and mercy – the wonderfully rich Hebrew word 'chesed' – that the people of Israel are today settled again in their own land, in fulfilment of prophecy. As the Jewish nation goes about its daily life, foreigners of all shapes and sizes are to be seen everywhere alongside Israelis. They work on construction sites, care for the elderly, harvest fruit, clean homes and look after children. Guest workers from Asia, Africa and Eastern Europe, or volunteers from Western nations, they have come to the Lord's land for various reasons, but all are serving the people of Israel just as Isaiah prophesied! All have joined themselves to Israel for a season and share in the trials and blessings of life in 'the land of the Lord', whether they acknowledge Him or not.

Did you notice that Isaiah actually says the land has two owners? In verse 1, it is Israel; and in verse 2, the Lord. Both of these are true of course, and confirmed by other parts of Scripture (eg Amos 9:15, Ezekiel 37:21, Leviticus 25:23, Deuteronomy 32:43, Joel 3:2). It is interesting to note however that when referring to Gentiles in verse 2, God's ownership is stressed. The land of Israel is especially significant in God's purposes not only for the Jewish people, but also for the peoples of the entire earth.

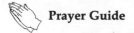 **Prayer Guide**

Praise God that His hand has miraculously gathered millions of Jews and resettled them in their own land, over the last century. Ask Him to bring many more, and help those still returning daily from many nations, to settle quickly and adjust to the very different way of life in Israel. '"*I will bring back the captives of My people Israel; They shall build the waste cities and inhabit them; they shall plant vineyards and drink wine from them; they shall also make gardens and eat fruit from them. I will plant them in their land, and no longer shall they be pulled up from the land I have given them," says the* LORD *your God'* (Amos 9:14, 15).

Thank God for the way He has used Gentiles, and especially Christians who believe His word, to help in this ingathering from its beginning. Pray that the various ministries in Israel and the nations who are busy helping the Jewish people return and resettle, will be prospered in their work. '*I will bless those who bless you, . . .*' (Genesis 12:3).

Pray for the foreign workers in Israel, that God's purpose in calling them there for a season will be fulfilled. Give thanks for the many outreaches to them, and for those from many nations who have come to faith in the God of Israel through Messiah Jesus. Pray that they may provoke many Israelis to jealousy through their love, life and witness.

> *'. . . Israel will be one of three with Egypt and Assyria – a blessing in the midst of the land, whom the LORD of hosts shall bless, saying, "Blessed is Egypt My people, and Assyria the work of My hands, and Israel My inheritance"'* (Isaiah 19:24, 25).

 Passage for study and prayer: Isaiah 19:16–25

'But what about the Palestinians? Doesn't God love the Arabs just as much as He loves the Jews?' This is a frequently asked question when discussing the restoration of Israel – and praise God, the answer is a resounding YES! God has no favourites, and He has His own 'road map' that will finally bring peace and blessing to all the peoples of the Middle East. Here Isaiah speaks of God raising up a highway between Egypt and Assyria, who, together with Israel, will form an axis of blessing for the whole region. The ancient Assyrian Empire encompassed modern Syria, Lebanon, northern Iraq and parts of Jordan and Turkey. Including Egypt, this is all of Israel's neighbours. Note that although now predominantly Muslim, all these countries have Christian minorities tracing their roots to the earliest times, who have remained a faithful witness to the true God, albeit often timidly in the face of persecution.

The Lord's plan is to restore the knowledge of Himself in these nations, where the early church began. However, he must bring judgement before He brings healing, and God's instrument of judgement is Israel (v17). God will strike Egypt, in order to heal her (v22). In the midst of the coming terror and destruction, those who know Him will be a sign and witness, and will point their compatriots to the Lord, who will deliver them through His Saviour, the Mighty One. In Hebrew, the word 'Saviour' is 'yasha', the root of the name Yeshua, or Jesus in English. Yeshua the Messiah is the Prince of Peace. The very turmoil and suffering in the Middle East will ultimately lead to the growth of His Kingdom, bringing reconciliation and blessing in its wake. Middle Eastern Christians are as vital a part of this plan as are the people of Israel, and also face great spiritual warfare. They need our fervent prayers too. Sadly, the resurgence of militant Islam in response to the return of the Jews has led to a mass emigration of Arab Christians to the West in recent decades.

 Prayer Guide

Pray fervently for the remaining Arab believers to be strengthened in their love and witness for Jesus, and have an understanding of His purposes for them. *'In that day there will be an altar to the LORD in the midst of the land of Egypt, and a pillar to the LORD at its border. And it will be for a sign and for a witness to the LORD of hosts . . .'* (vv19, 20).

Cry out with all your heart that the many serious problems facing people in the Arab Muslim world will lead to their swift, and full, salvation. *'. . . for they will cry to the LORD because of the oppressors, and He will send them a Saviour and a Mighty One, and He will deliver them'* (v20). Pray for God to bless and guide all ministries reaching out to them, and make them agents for reconciliation rather than division.

Pray fervently for the fulfilment of this promise that old enmities and rivalries within the Arab world will be forgotten and there will be unity and co-operation between them, as well as with Israel, in God's New Middle East. *'In that day there will be a highway from Egypt to Assyria, and the Assyrian will come into Egypt and the Egyptian into Assyria, and the Egyptians will serve with the Assyrians'* (v23).

THE VALLEY OF VISION

> *'For it is a day of trouble and treading down and perplexity by the Lord GOD of hosts in the Valley of Vision – breaking down the walls and of crying to the mountain'* (Isaiah 22:5).

 Passage for study and prayer: Isaiah 22:1–14

What is the Valley of Vision? The Hebrew word 'gah'ee', means gorge or steep-sided valley, and 'chizzayon' is a divine revelation. Whilst the context makes it clear that the prophet is referring to the literal valleys around Jerusalem in a specific historical situation, it is also obvious that his words carry a deeper spiritual meaning too. As so often in Scripture, the Lord is placing his people in a narrow and difficult place to try to speak to them, but alas they are not listening.

It is a situation that causes great anguish to Isaiah, who as an intercessor feels the heart of the Lord for His people (v4). Judah is in great trouble, because the Lord God of hosts has removed their spiritual covering (v8). In trying to flee, her rulers have been killed or taken captive (vv2, 3). Jerusalem is under siege, without effective leadership, and her desperate citizens are trying everything they can think of to find weapons, store water, even breaking down houses in an attempt to fortify the walls – but not doing the only really necessary and effective thing, which is to turn to their God who provided it all in the first place (vv9–11)! God was calling them to fasting and weeping in repentance, but instead, they did the opposite, living it up in a frantic, fatalistic attempt to escape their dire situation (vv12, 13). The Lord has no alternative but to allow judgement to overtake them, as He makes clear to Isaiah (v14).

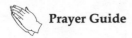 **Prayer Guide**

Intercede for the people of Israel today as they again face a time of trouble and treading down and perplexity, and the temptation is to try to find human solutions to their many problems. *'You also made a reservoir between the two walls for the water of the old pool. But you did not look to its Maker, nor did you have respect for Him who fashioned it long ago'* (v11). Pray for both leaders and people to see the futility of their own efforts and seek God's help, and have ears to hear His voice and hearts to obey Him.

Pray for God's Spirit to bring true conviction and repentance to the people of Israel concerning the many ways they have failed to live according to God's standards. *'And in that day the Lord GOD of hosts called for weeping and for mourning, . . .'* (v12). Beseech Him to maintain His covering and protection over them, and in judgement, to remember mercy.

Ask the Lord to give you His heart for His people, so that like Isaiah, you will be able to travail in prayer for them. *'Therefore I said, "Look away from me, I will weep bitterly; do not labour to comfort me because of the plundering of the daughter of my people"'* (v4). May He reveal to you and other intercessors how He is dealing with Israel so that you can pray effectively. *'Then it was revealed in my hearing by the LORD of hosts, . . .'* (v14).

IN AND OUT OF OFFICE

> *'So I will drive you [Shebna] out of your office, and from your position he will pull you down. Then . . . I will call My servant Eliakim the son of Hilkiah; I will clothe him with your robe and strengthen him with your belt; I will commit your responsibility into his hand'* (Isaiah 22:19–21).

 Passage for study and prayer: Isaiah 22:15–25

Israelis are used to elections. They go to the polls often, partly because their highly democratic system of government, allowing one man one vote for all citizens regardless of ethnic background, and exact proportional representation in the Knesset (parliament) according to the number of votes, leads to the proliferation of small parties. This means coalitions are the order of the day and governments are unstable and easy to bring down under pressure from one or other side of the political spectrum. Sadly, the system also lends itself to abuse as leaders often have to make concessions to try and stay in power, and others wield disproportionate influence tending to corruption and self-interest. The same is true at local government level throughout the country.

This passage gives us some great principles and guidelines for prayer in the light of this. Firstly, it shows us that the One behind all ins and outs of public office is the Lord Himself. He brings one down, and sets up another. Secondly, it shows us that He judges those with responsibility according to how they handle it. It seems clear that Shebna was removed from his position because he was using it to exalt himself in pride, to become powerful and amass great wealth. Thirdly, we find what the Lord wants those who govern to be like. Eliakim, as a humble man, will be a father to God's people, concerned for their welfare and ruling accordingly. As a result, he will be given great authority and influence and will be prospered in fulfilling his responsibilities, thus helping to fulfil God's purposes for the nation.

 Prayer Guide

Praise God that those who hold public office in Israel (and in your own country) are actually accountable to Him! Pray that He will remove those who are abusing their positions and not governing according to His righteous principles. *'Indeed, the LORD will throw you away violently, O mighty man, . . .' (v17).*

Ask Him to raise up men of humility and integrity in their place who will be His servants to lead the nation according to His heart. *'. . . He shall be a father to the inhabitants of Jerusalem and to the house of Judah' (v21).*

Earnestly pray for the current leaders of Israel to put the welfare of the nation above that of their own personal or party interests. Pray for wisdom and strength for them in the huge challenges they face, and beseech the Lord to use them to fulfil His perfect plan for Israel. *'The key of the house of David I will lay on his shoulder; so he shall open, and no one shall shut; and he shall shut, and no one shall open' (v22).*

A CALL TO THE SOUTH

> *'I will say to the north, "Give them up!" and to the south, "Do not keep them back!" Bring My sons from afar, and My daughters from the ends of the earth —"'* (Isaiah 43:6).

 Passage for study and prayer: Isaiah 43:1–7

Ethiopia lies south of Jerusalem, where Isaiah prophesied. Until recently this nation contained one of the most ancient Jewish communities in the world, claiming direct descent from King Solomon through the Queen of Sheba (1 Kings 10). Unlike other Diaspora Jews, they still observed many Torah rituals and sacrifices, showing that they had been in existence since even before the first exile to Babylon, let alone before the final destruction of the Temple in AD 70 led to the rise of modern rabbinical Judaism. Although living in simple village communities, often in great poverty and ostracised by their fellow Ethiopians, they kept a distinct identity and like all Jews, their hope and great desire over the centuries was to return to Jerusalem.

Even after Israel was created and the authenticity of Ethiopian Jewry confirmed, this seemed impossible. The communist regime in Ethiopia would not release them. However, God's word was impossible to resist! A few began to trickle back, and when the historic airlifts of Operations Moses and Solomon finally brought tens of thousands of Ethiopian Jews to Israel in the last decades of the twentieth century, the nation rejoiced. A new, vibrant culture was added to the mix that is modern Israel, bringing unique skills and attitudes and a fresh emphasis on many of the values of the Bible. There have been many struggles adjusting to a modern technological society in place of African village culture, but the new generation of

Ethiopian immigrants are finding their place and making a positive contribution to the life of the nation.

 Prayer Guide

Praise God for miraculously returning the Ethiopian Jews to the land and people of Israel, in fulfilment of prophecy. Pray that thousands more 'Falash Mura' (Jews who converted to Christianity generations ago but kept their Jewish identity) may be released to come, and pray for their physical and spiritual blessing in the land. *'Fear not, for I have redeemed you; I have called you by your name; you are Mine'* (v1).

Pray for the Lord's special grace and help for adult Ethiopians with the very difficult tasks of language learning and integration into complex Israeli society, and for those working to help them. *'When you pass through the waters, I will be with you; and through the rivers, they shall not overflow you . . .'* (v2). Pray for the children and young people, who often integrate more easily via the school system and army – but then face a 'generation gap' separating them from parents and community.

Thank God for the precious values of humility, gentleness, family loyalty and faith in God found in abundance in the Ethiopian community. Pray that these values will not be lost but rather shared, and that 'black Jews' will know the love of God in the face of occasional racism and discrimination. *'Since you were precious in My sight, you have been honoured, and I have loved you; . . .'* (v4).

SAVE THE CHILDREN

> *'But thus says the LORD: "Even the captives of the mighty shall be taken away, and the prey of the terrible be delivered; for I will contend with him who contends with you, and I will save your children"'* (Isaiah 49:25).

 Passage for study and prayer: Isaiah 49:14–26

One of the most devastating consequences of the ongoing Israeli-Palestinian conflict, especially in recent years, has been the effect on all the children. A whole generation is growing up in fear, knowing that their lives could change in an instant as a result of random terror attacks. Family outings to restaurants, bus rides from school, or drives to visit friends and relatives in other towns could end in sudden death and destruction. Hundreds of youngsters have lost their lives. Many hundreds more have been maimed for life, or lost parents or siblings – almost all are marked psychologically. There is hardly a family in Israel untouched by the conflict. The situation for Palestinian youngsters is equally traumatic. Not only do they suffer the fearful consequences of ongoing military action against terror, they are systematically brainwashed via the Palestinian media and schools to desire death as a 'shahid' or martyr. Young people on both sides are being brutalised by the horrors of war.

Satan is always out to destroy the coming generation, but perhaps this generation in particular, as signs point to the soon return of the Messiah. He tried hard before Israel was reborn, with well over a million Jewish children perishing in the Holocaust – but some were saved by Gentiles and later brought to Israel in ways foreshadowed in this passage (vv22, 23). Praise God He has pledged to take on the one who strives against His people! His power is far greater than the most ruthless or terrible enemy, and He has promised deliverance and salvation for Israel's children. The word used here for save is 'yasha' – the root from which the name Yeshua (in English, Jesus) comes (Matthew 1:21). Is not God's purpose, as in any situation of suffering, to use it to draw people to the source of their only true salvation and deliverance, Israelis and Palestinians alike?

 Prayer Guide

Stand in the gap for Israel's youngsters today, praying earnestly for their protection and release from all the efforts of the enemy to ensnare them and destroy their lives, physically, emotionally and spiritually. *'Shall the prey be taken from the mighty, or the captives of the righteous be delivered?'* (v24). Yes! God has promised it.

Pray especially for healing for those who have been traumatised by terror. *'For the LORD has comforted His people, and will have mercy on His afflicted'* (v13b). Especially remember the many who have been permanently mutilated, and have to live with handicaps for the rest of their lives, and their families and caregivers. May they come to know Him through their suffering: *'. . . Then you will know that I am the LORD, for they shall not be ashamed who wait for Me'* (v23).

Pray for all efforts to bring Jewish and Arab children together to teach mutual understanding and curb hatred. Above all, pray for true and lasting reconciliation through Messiah, to be a powerful witness to the world. Especially pray for young believers to be a witness to their peers of His love and power. *'All flesh shall know that I, the LORD, am your Saviour, and your Redeemer, the Mighty One of Jacob'* (v26b).

GOD'S WAYS ARE NOT OURS

> *'For My thoughts are not your thoughts, nor are your ways My ways,' says the LORD. 'For as the heavens are higher than the earth, so are My ways higher than your ways, and My thoughts than your thoughts'* (Isaiah 55:8, 9).

 Passage for study and prayer: Isaiah 55

How many times in your Christian life have you discovered that God's ways and thoughts are not yours? It is one of the hardest lessons to learn, because our thinking is so conditioned by our culture and education. Until we know better, we think the same way as the vast majority of those around us, without ever questioning, and often behave accordingly. How much blessing we miss and how much agony we suffer because of it!

When it comes to the subject of Israel, this problem looms large. Humanism rules in most Western minds. This thinking is man-centred and has no place for God. The absolute values of right and wrong are replaced by relative morality, and tolerance and compromise are elevated to the highest of virtues. Humanism, based on Greek thinking, conflicts head on with the Bible and the Lord's plans for Israel and the nations. Sadly, such views find a ready audience in much of the church too.

God's thoughts are often difficult to understand from a lowly, worldly viewpoint, but they are always governed by His love. This passage clearly shows that listening to His word and submitting to it always brings blessing and fruitfulness, both individual and corporate, as well as glory to His name. We don't have to understand in order to believe and obey. Whilst the conventional wisdom concerning Israel is shaped by humanism at best and the implacable hostility of demonic anti-Semitism at worst, we have God's word as our guide and only authority. That is why Paul exhorts us in Romans 12:2 to renew our minds through obedience to Scripture, rather than be squeezed into the world's mould!

 Prayer Guide

Praise God that His thoughts and ways are always true, always righteous, always dependable! Declare in faith that His Word and promises for His people shall surely be fulfilled in due season. *'For as the rain comes down, and the snow from heaven, and . . . water the earth, and make it bring forth and bud, that it may give seed to the sower and bread to the eater, so shall My word be that goes forth from My mouth; it shall not return to Me void, but it shall accomplish what I please, and it shall prosper in the thing for which I sent it'* (vv10, 11).

Pray through this passage verse by verse on behalf of the Jewish people. Pray that they will hear the word of the Lord and turn back to Him in repentance and obedience, that their souls may live. *'Incline your ear, and come to Me. Hear, and your soul shall live; and I will make an everlasting covenant with you – the sure mercies of David'* (v3).

Pray the same for Gentiles, who are given the way into covenant relationship with God and adoption into His people through the Messiah, Son of David. *'Let the wicked forsake his way, and the unrighteous man his thoughts; let him return to the LORD, and He will have mercy on him; . . .'* (v7). Pray especially that as Christians we will be released from humanistic thinking and be transformed through the renewing of our minds, so that we may perceive God's true purposes for Israel in our day.

REPAIRER OF THE BREACH

'Those from among you shall build the old waste places; you shall raise up the foundations of many generations; and you shall be called the Repairer of the Breach, the Restorer of Streets to Dwell In' (Isaiah 58:12).

 Passage for study and prayer: Isaiah 58:9–12

God first gave these wonderful words of promise to the people of Israel. Today they are still for them, but also for Christian believers, grafted in by faith in the Jewish Messiah to the covenants of God. As with so many of God's promises, they are conditional, but if we fulfil the conditions, we are promised not only His guidance, provision and strength, but also the privilege of involvement in His work of restoration. We will be among those who will build the old waste places in the spiritual realm – just as on the natural level, there are those of the people of Israel who have rebuilt in the very places where previous communities stood, in fulfilment of prophecy. (See also Jeremiah 31.)

Although Israel continues to be restored physically day by day, that restoration will mean nothing, apart from God's parallel work of spiritual restoration to Himself and His word. That is the work we share in through our faithful intercession. Generations to come will be affected by the impact of our prayers, restoring and rebuilding the purposes of God. As we meditate on this passage, let us turn it into prayer, both for ourselves and for the people of Israel.

Sadly, despite the traditional Jewish emphasis on righteous deeds and caring for those in need, there are many instances of self-seeking factionalism, oppression of the weak and neglect of the poor in Israel today.

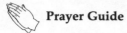 **Prayer Guide**

Earnestly pray that both government and individuals will be convicted of these sins, and the need to live according to God's word. *'If you take away the yoke from your midst, the pointing of the finger, and speaking wickedness, if you extend your soul to the hungry and satisfy the afflicted soul, then your light shall dawn in the darkness, and your darkness shall be as the noonday'* (vv9b, 10).

Seek God's mercy upon Israel in the light of this passage. Ask Him to bless and prosper all those who are fulfilling these conditions, and grant them guidance and strength. As Israel faces times of great darkness and tragedy, may He fulfil His promise and provide refreshing in the midst of suffering: *'The LORD will guide you continually, and satisfy your soul in drought, and strengthen your bones; you shall be like a watered garden, and like a spring of water, whose waters do not fail'* (v11).

Thank the Lord for all those He is using to repair the breaches and restore the ancient dwelling places, both physically and spiritually, and pray for wisdom, strength and persever-ance for them in the face of many obstacles. Seek God's anointing for your own role as an intercessor for Israel, that your prayers may be effective in laying strong foundations for the future.

THE THRONE OF THE LORD

> 'At that time Jerusalem shall be called The Throne of the LORD, and all the nations shall be gathered to it, to the name of the LORD, to Jerusalem. No more shall they follow the dictates of their evil hearts' (Jeremiah 3:17).

 Passage for study and prayer: Jeremiah 3:6–18

These verses are amongst the most amazing prophecies in Scripture. Jeremiah sees far into the future, to the time when the Ark of the Covenant will cease to be the symbol of the presence of the Lord for the people of Israel. Instead, Jerusalem itself will become God's throne, His seat of power, and the place where His presence dwells – the focal point not only for Israel but all the nations of the earth.

We know that this will only be finally fulfilled when the New Jerusalem comes down from heaven, as John describes in the book of Revelation. But the context relates this event to a number of other circumstances that are in the process of happening even today. The return of a remnant of Jews to Zion has been very clearly fulfilled in past centuries, and especially after the Holocaust (v14). The people of Israel have multiplied and increased in the land since then, and shepherds according to His heart are being raised up to bring true spiritual understanding (v15). Above all, the Lord's heart cry is heard throughout this passage – 'Return to Me' (vv7, 12, 14). The purpose of it all is to bring the children of Israel away from their backsliding and into real repentance and renewed relationship with their God, who is eternally and irrevocably committed to His people.

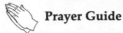 **Prayer Guide**

Give thanks for the faithfulness and mercy of the Lord, who longs to show love to the backslider. '. . . *Return, backsliding Israel,' says the LORD; 'I will not cause My anger to fall on you. For I am merciful . . . I will not remain angry forever. Return, O backsliding children, . . . for I am married to you'* (vv12, 14). Pray for a powerful spirit of repentance to fall on the people of Israel for their many forms of idolatry and disobedience. *'"Only acknowledge your iniquity, that you have transgressed against the LORD your God, . . . and you have not obeyed My voice," says the LORD'* (v13).

Beseech the Lord to raise up true shepherds (pastors) to lead His people into God's ways, as He promised. *'And I will give you shepherds according to My heart, who will feed you with knowledge and understanding'* (v15). May those who have seeking hearts not be deceived by false teachings and doctrines such as the New Age, humanism etc but rather be guided to the truth of His entire Word.

Praise God for the re-gathering of Israel from different countries and pray for their forging, by the Spirit of God, into one united people. *'In those days the house of Judah shall walk with the house of Israel, and they shall come together out of the land of the north to the land that I have given as an inheritance to your fathers'* (v18). Above all, pray for the fulfilment of God's purposes for Jerusalem as the place where all the nations will be drawn to experience His presence and sovereign rule.

A FOUNTAIN OF TEARS

> *'Oh, that my head were waters, and my eyes a fountain of tears, that I might weep day and night for the slain of the daughter of my people!'* (Jeremiah 9:1)

 Passage for study and prayer: Jeremiah 8:15–9:1

Today there are many in Israel for whom these words of Jeremiah are a very real heart's cry. Since the 'Oslo Accords' of the 1990s disappeared in a welter of blood at the outbreak of the second Palestinian uprising in September 2000, hundreds of Israelis have been killed and thousands more injured in terror attacks. Israel is family – when someone dies, the whole nation mourns, and weeps with those who weep.

One group in particular has borne the brunt of the grief and pain of the nation, and that is Israel's medical and emergency services. Her world-class hospitals offer expert medical care not only to Israeli citizens both Jewish and Arab, but to Palestinians too. Jewish and Arab Israeli doctors work side by side to tend the victims of violence.

Paradoxically, the rash of suicide bombings has led to great advances in the field of trauma medicine as doctors learn more about blast injuries and surgery to remove lethal shrapnel from vital organs. However, the sheer number of emergency cases and serious injuries has placed great strain on medical and rehabilitation services. The resources of Israel's 'Red Shield', Magen David Adom, have also been stretched to the limit. All those who have attended multiple tragedies over many months or treated the victims are profoundly affected emotionally by what they have seen and felt.

This passage shows that the experience is nothing new for God's people. So often when they have expected the peace they long for, violence and strife have come instead. God says clearly that He allows pain as part of His discipline and judgement. However, there are also many promises of His own healing and comfort, when His people look to Him.

 Prayer Guide

Pray for the people of Israel in their pain and bitter disappointment at yet again finding peace efforts turning to ashes. *'We looked for peace, but no good came; and for a time of health, and there was trouble!'* (v15). Pray that their sufferings may cause them to ask questions and seek God for the answers; *'Listen! The voice, the cry of the daughter of my people from a far country: "Is not the LORD in Zion? Is not her King in her?"'* (v19).

Pray for strength and healing for the medical and emergency personnel who are weary and traumatised after responding to years of violence and terror, when every patient could be their own son or daughter, parent or friend. *'I would comfort myself in sorrow; my heart is faint in me. For the hurt of the daughter of my people I am hurt. I am mourning; astonishment has taken hold of me'* (vv18, 21).

Give thanks for Israel's fine hospitals, rehabilitation centres and ambulance service that serve all patients without discrimination. Ask the Lord to supply all needed resources. *'Is there no balm in Gilead, is there no physician there? Why then is there no recovery for the health of the daughter of my people?'* (v22). May they also be centres of true hope and reconciliation.

Pray for God's divine healing power to be released through all those who minister to the sick and injured. *'[The LORD] heals the brokenhearted and binds up their wounds'* (Psalm 147:3).

DRAWN OR DRIVEN

> *'Behold, I will send for many fishermen' says the* LORD, *'and they shall fish them; and afterward I will send for many hunters, and they shall hunt them from every mountain and every hill, and out of the holes of the rocks'* (Jeremiah 16:16).

 Passage for study and prayer: Jeremiah 16:14–21

In God's mercy and grace, He always tries the lure before the weapon in moving His people into the place of blessing and restoration. The worm on the hook, the fly on the surface of the waters – these are powerful inducements to the fish to bite and be drawn into the hand of the fisherman. For those who won't be drawn, the alternative is to be driven. The second image is of creatures flushed out from every hiding place by relentless hunters, weapons in hand, forced into the will of the Lord.

The context of this passage is the return of the people of Israel to their homeland, after a time of severe punishment for their gross sins against the Lord and His word. Their idolatry will lead to a violent casting out of their land. However, in the midst of pronouncing this judgement, God promises He will bring them back from exile in the future, in a way that will be even more for His glory than their original deliverance from Egypt. He will use first fishers, then hunters, to drive them back to their land and into His purposes. Israel's recent history abounds with examples of this principle, from the early Zionists fleeing the pogroms of Russia in the 1890s to the rebirth of Israel as a nation out of the ashes of the Holocaust in 1948. In recent years, the fishers have been busy contributing to a surge of immigration into Israel – but as the tide of anti-Semitism rises worldwide, God is once more using the hunters to drive His people back to their only refuge, the place He has appointed for them.

 Prayer Guide

Praise God for the modern miracle of over a million new immigrants since 1989 from the nations of the Former Soviet Union, after communism collapsed and the doors opened. *'The LORD lives who brought up the children of Israel from the land of the north and from all the lands where He had driven them'* (v15a). Pray for the continuing 'aliyah' (ingathering) from the land of the north and all the nations where Jews now live. *'For I will bring them back into their land which I gave to their fathers'* (v15b). As anti-Semitism in its new guise of anti-Zionism grows ever stronger, pray fervently for the Jewish people to read the warning signs and return to Zion before it is too late.

Ask God to preserve a large remnant and pray for many to be raised up, especially Christians, to love them and help them escape from their persecutors.

Give thanks that God sees both the sin and the suffering of the Jewish people, and that even though he punishes them for their failure to honour all He has given them, He will never abandon them or His purposes for them. *'For My eyes are on all their ways; they are not hidden from My face, nor is their iniquity hidden from My eyes. And first I will repay double for their iniquity and their sin, because they have defiled My land;'* (vv17, 18a). Pray that the suffering still to come will bring them into the very centre of His will for their individual and corporate lives.

A point to ponder – will we be drawn or driven in our own lives?

THE RIGHT OF INHERITANCE

> 'Then Hanamel my uncle's son came to me in the court of the prison according to the word of the LORD, and said to me, "Please buy my field that is in Anathoth, which is in the country of Benjamin; for the right of inheritance is yours, and the redemption yours; buy it for yourself." Then I knew that this was the word of the LORD' (Jeremiah 32:8).

 Passage for study and prayer: Jeremiah 32

Jeremiah was not surprised when his cousin visited him to ask him to redeem his inheritance, even though the request seemed ridiculous – the prophet was in prison, Jerusalem was besieged, and destruction of the temple and exile in Babylon was just around the corner. The Lord had forewarned him (vv6, 7), so Hanamel's appearance was simply a confirmation. Jeremiah did not hesitate to obey God's instructions, paying the purchase price and observing the legal requirements to redeem the land of his inheritance. His costly action was a prophetic sign of future restoration (v15).

But although he was obedient, Jeremiah was still rather confused. How did all this tie in with what was happening right outside the prison doors, here and now? He prayed for further understanding, and the Lord answered with more revelation. He showed him that the present suffering had a redemptive purpose; and that the restoration of His people to their physical inheritance, would lead to renewal of their bridal relationship with Himself in an everlasting covenant (v40). His unfailing love governs all. Today, this is equally true. In the process of restoration, Israel is again under siege and experiencing great trauma and suffering. Her enemies seek to destroy her and claim her inheritance, but God's word will prevail. We have to see that in seemingly impossible circumstances, the Lord is working out the redemption of not only His people, but also all mankind.

 Prayer Guide

Praise God that since the beginning of the restoration of Israel, every major effort of her enemies to remove her inheritance has ultimately resulted in the redeeming of more of her territory. Proclaim God's word by faith: *'"Men will buy fields for money, sign deeds and seal them, and take witnesses, in the land of Benjamin [Judea], in the places around Jerusalem, in the cities of Judah [Judea], in the cities of the mountains [Samaria and Golan], in the cities of the lowland [coastal plain and Gaza], and in the cities of the South [Negev]; for I will cause their captives to return," says the LORD'* (v44).

Wrestle in prayer that the result of all the sufferings for both Jews and Palestinians in the land today will lead to a great salvation and reconciliation of both peoples to the God of Israel and His Messiah. *'Behold, I am the LORD, the God of all flesh. Is there anything too hard for Me?'* (v27).

Rejoice with Jeremiah in the wonderful attributes of God listed in verses 17–22. Declare His power over all the darkness Israel faces today, and pray for the fulfilment of the wonderful promises of peace, reconciliation, safety and blessing detailed in verses 37–42.

HEART TRANSPLANT

> *'I will give them an undivided heart and put a new spirit in them; I will remove from them their heart of stone and give them a heart of flesh'* (Ezekiel 11:19 NIV).

 Passage for study and prayer: Ezekiel 11:14–21

Ezekiel was given this prophecy while in exile in Babylon. At this stage, many Jews remained in Jerusalem, and they criticised those who had been taken into captivity, believing that God had given them the land and they would therefore remain in it (v15). They did not see their sin. The Lord made it clear that those who suffered the punishment would come to know the Lord even in their captivity (v16) and would be restored to their land in due time (v17). When that happened, they would receive much more than just the land – they would be given the opportunity to destroy the idols surrounding them and receive a new heart and spirit.

Since the modern Zionist movement began in the 1880s, Jews have been fulfilling this prophecy and returning in large numbers to their ancestral homeland. Literally millions have been transplanted from many nations into their native soil. But God's ultimate purpose in bringing them back goes far beyond mere revival of their ancient nation. As Ezekiel spells out, Israel was founded so that the Lord could perform another kind of transplant, involving the Jewish heart.

For over 2,000 years the people of Israel were a persecuted minority in many nations, without responsibilities of government. As such they became acutely conscious of human rights and the high moral values enshrined in the Torah, their Holy Scriptures, which gave them cohesion as a people. Now after more than 50 years of statehood they are finding that the grim realities of government, especially as they face implacable hostility from their enemies, lead to many unpleasant responsibilities that often prick their tender consciences. This is all part of God's plan to show them the desperate state of their own hearts, and lead them in both His judgement and His mercy, to the place where they cry out to Him for a new heart and spirit.

 Prayer Guide

Praise God that all His dealings with His people are designed to be redemptive, and that He will never forsake them even in the midst of chastising them for their iniquity. '. . . *Although I sent them far away among the nations and scattered them among the countries, yet for a little while I have been a sanctuary for them in the countries where they have gone'* (v16).

Pray earnestly for a renewed commitment to the righteous standards of the Torah on the part of Israelis, both in public and private life. Pray that new immigrants to Israel from many nations will have an impact for good in their society, and encourage higher standards. '. . . *I will gather you from the nations . . . and I will give you back the land of Israel again. They will return to it and remove all its vile images and detestable idols'* (vv17, 18).

Pray for the Lord Himself to soften individual Jewish hearts to His Word, both in Israel and the Diaspora, and bring conviction of sin and a desire to know Him and to receive His Messiah. *'Then they will follow my decrees and be careful to keep my laws. They will be my people, and I will be their God'* (v20). May the conflicts and questions that many Jewish people have today lead them back to God's Word, and show them their need of a Saviour.

STANDING IN THE GAP

> *'So I sought for a man among them who would make a wall, and stand in the gap before Me on behalf of the land, that I should not destroy it; but I found no one'* (Ezekiel 22:30).

 Passage for study and prayer: Ezekiel 22:23–31

God's cry is for an intercessor. He searched for just one person who would share His heart of love, His horror at the gross sins of His people, His burden for His own land so that He would not have to destroy it. The last thing the Lord wants to do is to give His people up to the consequences of their own behaviour. His loving heart would so much rather avoid it, but He must satisfy justice and the terms of His covenant. What is His way out of this heartbreaking situation?

This extraordinary passage shows that the Lord is actively looking for a righteous person who is willing to give of himself sacrificially to plug a gap or cover a breach in a defensive wall. The picture here is of a nation so steeped in sin that the very land is dried up and lifeless. The leaders – prophets, priests and secular rulers – have all utterly failed the people, who themselves have oppressed one another and the strangers in their midst. These terrible sins make a hole in their spiritual covering, which must somehow be bridged if God is not to deal with them as they deserve. Sadly, in this case, there was no one to intercede or literally 'stand between' and the judgement fell.

Of course verse 30 points forward prophetically to the only One who was truly able to stand in the gap and take our deserved judgement upon Himself in His own body – but we, as His servants, are also called to share in His work of intercession. Will we stand in the gap, sacrificially, for Israel and help maintain her spiritual covering?

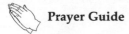 **Prayer Guide**

Thank God for the privilege of standing in the gap for Israel and pray for His strength and anointing to carry out this often demanding and sacrificial task. Pray that the Lord will find a multitude of intercessors to help maintain the spiritual covering over the nation in the coming days.

Pray especially for the believers in Israel – Jewish, Arab and those from the nations who are there by command of the Lord. Lift them up as they seek to be salt and light in their society. May they be used powerfully to make up the hedge of protection around Israel, through their prayers, faith, and love. *'For this reason we also, . . . do not cease to pray for you, and to ask that you may be filled with the knowledge of His will in all wisdom and spiritual understanding;'* (Colossians 1:9).

Pray diligently for those who give moral and religious direction to the people, such as rabbis, academics and those in the media, that they may not fail in their duty to guide Israel according to God's principles. *'Her priests have violated My law and profaned My holy things; they have not distinguished between the holy and unholy, nor have they made known the difference between the unclean and the clean; . . .'* (v26).

THE MOUNTAINS OF ISRAEL

> *'And you, son of man, prophesy to the mountains of Israel,
> and say, "O mountains of Israel, hear the word of the LORD!"'*
> (Ezekiel 36:1).

 Passage for study and prayer: Ezekiel 36:1–15

These mountains form the backbone of the most hotly con-
tested piece of real estate in the world, except Jerusalem itself,
known to the world as the West Bank. Israel uses the biblical
names of Judea in the south, and Samaria, or Shomron, to the
north. They are the very heartland of biblical Israel, and are
dotted with the remains of ancient Jewish communities alongside Arab towns and villages. They are also seen as the greatest
stumbling block to peace in the region. Arabs insist that this is
part of their historical and religious homeland and must
become a Muslim Palestinian state that is 'Judenrein' (without
any Jews). Jews quote both biblical and historical reasons for
their legal right to settle there, and also fear that their future
security depends on it. These days, the real facts are so
obscured by propaganda and deeply felt emotion on all sides,
that even Christians have difficulty discerning the truth of it all.

Praise God, His word is unmistakably clear on the subject.
Firstly, these mountains belong to Him (v5). They are part of
His land, which He cares for passionately (v9). Secondly, He
has given them to His people Israel as part of their inheritance
(v12). Moreover, he is furious with the nations that have tried
to seize them, and made them the subject of gossip and slander. He will bring His people home to inhabit them, to restore
the ancient communities and make their hills and valleys fruit-
ful once again. This prophecy has already been partly fulfilled
in our day, as new towns and villages have risen on the ancient

ruins of biblical sites. Whatever the outcome of current politics, we know from these Scriptures that these mountains will be part of the restored nation of Israel at some time in the future, for God has said so. What is more, they will then bring blessing instead of bloodshed for *all* that live on them (v14). Truly the real battle is spiritual, although manifested politically with much suffering.

 Prayer Guide

Proclaim these verses in prayer and faith for fulfilment in God's perfect time. Pray for the lifting up of the name of the true God, the Father of our Lord Jesus, on these mountains, and the pulling down of all other spiritual strongholds that would set themselves against Him and His truth. '*. . . thus says the Lord GOD [YAHWEH]: "Surely I have spoken in My burning jealousy against the rest of the nations and against all Edom, who gave My land to themselves as a possession, . . ."*' (v5).

Beseech the Lord to bring His people home from the four corners of the earth to repopulate His land. '*But you, O mountains of Israel, you shall shoot forth your branches and yield your fruit to My people Israel, for they are about to come*' (v8). Pray for the protection and prosperity of Jewish communities already re-established on these mountains. '*I will multiply men upon you, all the house of Israel, all of it; and the cities shall be inhabited and the ruins rebuilt*' (v10).

Pray fervently for an end to all conflict and bloodshed, and for the blessing and prospering in peace, side by side, of all those God has placed on these mountains: '*"therefore you shall devour men no more, nor bereave your nation anymore," says the Lord GOD*' (v14).

FOR YOUR NAME'S SAKE

> *'. . . Thus says the Lord GOD: "I do not do this for your sake, O house of Israel, but for My holy name's sake, which you have profaned among the nations wherever you went. And I will sanctify My great name, which has been profaned among the nations, . . . and the nations shall know that I am the LORD . . ."'* (Ezekiel 36:22, 23).

 Passage for study and prayer: Ezekiel 36:16–38

Why is it so important that the anti-Semitic and militant Islamic voices arising in the world today to try to destroy Israel once and for all, do not succeed? It is neither because Israel is the most righteous nation on the face of the earth, nor because she is a tiny David facing the Goliath of huge and powerful Islamic nations allied against her. We do not pray for Israel's survival because we feel sorry for her, nor because we have stood at Israel's side as Christian Zionists for years and do not want to be proved wrong if the Jews are finally driven out of the Middle East. No, there are far more important and fundamental issues at stake which drive our fervent intercession and cause us to cry out to God on Israel's behalf. The issues concern the Lord Himself.

Behind all the forces arrayed against Israel is a Satanic enemy whose great desire is to prevent the fulfilment of God's word, prove the Bible a lie and the God of Israel powerless to save His people. The struggle in the Middle East is much more than the clash of two cultures or the problem of a land claimed by two peoples. It is first and foremost a spiritual conflict between the God of Israel who is the Father of our Lord Jesus and the God of the Bible, and the counterfeit religions of Islam and secular humanism. The character of God, even His very existence is being challenged. As He instructs us, we must urgently call on Him to act for His own name's sake, that His purposes to use Israel to reveal His glory to the nations may be fulfilled in our day.

 Prayer Guide

Pray fervently that God's name may be glorified in all that happens in Israel and the Middle East, so that the nations may know that God is the LORD (YHWH) when they see His mighty acts. *'And I will sanctify My great name, which has been profaned among the nations, which you have profaned in their midst; and the nations shall know that I am the LORD,' says the Lord GOD, 'when I am hallowed in you before their eyes'* (v23). Pray likewise that political developments will serve to pull down the strongholds of false religion and all who would set themselves up against God.

Pray for the lives of both Jews and Christians, who worship the God of Israel, to sanctify (make holy) His name as they live in consistency with His word. *'I will put My Spirit within you and cause you to walk in My statutes, and you will keep My judgments and do them'* (v27). Especially pray that Israel as a nation may conduct herself worthy of the Lord, whose very name is reflected in her name.

Give thanks that the restoration of Israel is a work of God, designed to be a witness to the nations. Pray through all the promises in this passage, asking God to fulfil them not only for Israel's sake, but for the extension of His kingdom worldwide, and especially in the Middle East. *'Then the nations which are left all around you shall know that I, the LORD, have rebuilt the ruined places and planted what was desolate. I, the LORD, have spoken it, and I will do it'* (v36).

UNDERSTANDING BY THE BOOKS

> '. . . in the first year of his reign I, Daniel, understood by the books the number of the years specified by the word of the LORD through Jeremiah the prophet, that He would accomplish seventy years in the desolations of Jerusalem' (Daniel 9:2).

 Passage for study and prayer: Daniel 9:1–22

What drove Daniel to pray one of the most heartfelt prayers recorded in the entire Bible? What led him to put aside all other activities for a season and seek the Lord diligently, with fasting, sackcloth and ashes? What brought him to such identification with his people and their sins that he made detailed confession to God and stood upon His character to plead powerfully for forgiveness and action? He gives us the answer himself – 'I understood from the books'. Daniel knew the Scriptures. He had read Jeremiah's prophecy, sent to Babylon almost 70 years earlier (Jeremiah 29:10). He knew it was God's plan to return the exiles from Babylon to Jerusalem, and he realised that the time was ripe for the fulfilment of His word.

Knowing all this, Daniel could have sat back and let God get on with it – after all, He had declared it as His purpose, and He was perfectly able to accomplish it. But he didn't. Instead, understanding God's plan galvanised him to prayerful action. He longed to see prophecy fulfilled, and would do all he could to help it happen. His love for his city and his people, and above all for the Lord whom he knew so well, drove him to his knees. In so doing, he provides a model prayer for intercessors, which has never been surpassed. What's more, as he prayed and worshipped, he gained even more understanding and revelation from the Lord (v22). God gives us the prophetic Scriptures specifically so that we may read them, understand them, and be a part of their fulfilment through our prayers.

 Prayer Guide

Seek the Lord for a greater understanding of His prophetic word about Israel, to help you pray more effectively. *'Then I set my face toward the Lord God to make request by prayer and supplications, with fasting, sackcloth and ashes. . . . "O Daniel, I have now come forth to give you skill to understand"'* (vv3, 22). Pray earnestly for God to give many in the church the burden to pray, leading to greater understanding and revelation.

Pray too for the people of Israel to seek God as Daniel did, acknowledge their sins and the truth of the word of God, and call on Him in prayer. *'As it is written in the Law of Moses, all this disaster has come upon us; yet we have not made our prayer before the LORD our God, that we might turn from our iniquities and understand Your truth'* (v13).

Praise and pray through Daniel's prayer on behalf of Israel and the Jewish people today. Proclaim God's faithfulness and mercy and whilst acknowledging their many sins and failures, beseech Him to act in forgiveness and salvation: *'O Lord, hear! O Lord, forgive! O Lord, listen and act! Do not delay for Your own sake, my God, for Your city and Your people are called by Your name'* (v19).

GOING WITH GOD'S PEOPLE

> *'This is what the* LORD *Almighty says: "In those days ten men from all languages and nations will take firm hold of one Jew by the hem of his robe and say, 'Let us go with you, because we have heard that God is with you'"'* (Zechariah 8:23 NIV).

 Passage for study and prayer: Zechariah 8:20–23

Here is an amazing and exciting prophecy of the end times. God says the day will come when ten men from all the nations of the world shall grab one Jew by the edge of his garment and say, 'We are going with you!' Instead of being despised and rejected, victimised and persecuted by those who consider themselves stronger and superior, people will jostle and compete to be alongside the Jew. Why? 'Because we have heard that God is with you.' This is the calling of the Jewish people, to lead the nations to God.

Not just any god, but specifically the LORD Almighty, or LORD of Hosts ('Sabaoth' in Hebrew). Watch for this – whenever the Bible has the word 'LORD' or 'GOD' in capitals, it indicates the four Hebrew letters YHWH, rendered Yahweh or Jehovah in English. (Jews never pronounce the sacred Name, but use 'Adonai' or Lord, instead when they speak of Him.) YHWH is the personal, covenant name for the God of Israel, indicating His eternal nature and character. The LORD can never be confused with any other gods, such as Allah, or Shiva, or Buddha. He is the One who has chosen Jerusalem for Himself, to put His name there (1 Kings 11:36), and all others are merely pretenders to His throne (Jeremiah 3:17). He is the one whom Jesus called Father, whom He worshipped and to whom He prayed. This is why the destiny of Jerusalem and the Jew is inextricably linked together with the final revelation to all men of the one true God and His returning Messiah.

 Prayer Guide

Declare in faith that '. . . *many peoples and strong nations shall come to seek the LORD of hosts in Jerusalem, and to pray before the LORD*' (v22 NKJV). Rejoice that the day is coming when He will have no rivals worshipped in the Holy City, and will be known to all by His covenant name of YHWH!

Pray for the fulfilment of the promise that the peoples of many cities will encourage each other to make the decision to seek the LORD Almighty personally in prayer. *'The inhabitants of one city shall go to another, saying, "Let us continue to go and pray before the LORD, and seek the LORD of hosts. I myself will go also"'* (v21 NKJV). Pray that it may happen in all the cities, towns and villages of Israel, for Jew and Arab and foreigner alike.

Pray earnestly for the Jewish people as they face much spiritual warfare aimed at thwarting this divine destiny for themselves and Jerusalem. Pray for their protection and for their spiritual preparation, especially that they may recognise their Messiah. Cry out for the perfect fulfilment of all God's prophetic purposes for Jerusalem.

CONDITIONS OF HIS COMING

> '*O Jerusalem, Jerusalem, the one who kills the prophets and stones those who are sent to her! How often I wanted to gather your children together, as a hen gathers her chicks under her wings, but you were not willing! See! Your house is left to you desolate; for I say to you, you shall see Me no more till you say, "Blessed is He who comes in the name of the LORD!"'*
> (Matthew 23:37–39).

 Passage for study and prayer: Matthew 23:29–24:14

Both Luke and Matthew record for us Jesus' heartbreak over his beloved city and people of Jerusalem, but only Matthew places this cry in the context of Jesus' final prophetic teaching concerning the end of the age. Jesus mourns because he knows what lies ahead, both for them and for Himself. The religious leaders are once again about to reject both God's word and His messenger, as they have done before, and the coming destruction will be the greatest yet. (Jesus' prophecy about the temple in Matthew 24:2 was literally fulfilled when the Roman armies breached the city in AD 70. The temple was set alight and the stones were torn apart as looters retrieved the melted gold that flowed down between the cracks.)

However, there is hope. 'Baruch haba b'shem Adonai' – 'Blessed is He who comes in the name of the Lord' – is the cry from Psalm 118:26 which, in Jewish tradition, is a plea for the Messiah to come in saving power. That same cry had been shouted as Jesus rode into Jerusalem just a few days before (Matthew 21:9)! Now He prophesies, 'You won't see me again until you once again herald me as Messiah.' Even before His death and resurrection, Jesus knew there would be a future, final return to His people – but it will not happen until they cry out with all their being for the Messiah to come and save them.

A little later, the disciples seek a fuller explanation of the signs of His final coming and end of the age. Jesus then gives another condition for His return – the preaching of the good news of God's kingdom to all peoples (v14). These two things will happen before He comes back to rule and reign in Jerusalem. We need to pray for both!

Prayer Guide

Give thanks that Jesus will return as King of Kings and Lord of Lords, just as He promised. *'Then the sign of the Son of Man will appear in heaven, and then all the tribes of the earth will mourn, and they will see the Son of Man coming on the clouds of heaven with power and great glory'* (24:30). Pray fervently for His people and His City, Jerusalem, to be ready for His coming. Ask God to stir a great desire in Jewish hearts to see their Messiah, and to cry out for His coming deliverance.

Pray for yourself and for all those who love Jesus and His Jewish brethren to be faithful to God and His Word, as opposition, temptation, deception and persecution will intensify in the coming days. *'And because lawlessness will abound, the love of many will grow cold. But he who endures to the end shall be saved'* (24:12, 13).

Pray for all ministries involved in world mission, especially those focusing on unreached peoples. Beseech the Lord to fulfil His plan for world evangelisation through Israel and the Church. *'And this gospel of the kingdom will be preached in all the world as a witness to all the nations, and then the end will come'* (24:14).

THE TWO BROTHERS

> *'Now his older son was in the field. And as he came and drew near to the house, he heard music and dancing. So he called one of the servants and asked what these things meant. And he said to him, "Your brother has come, and because he has received him safe and sound, your father has killed the fatted calf." But he was angry and would not go in. Therefore his father came out and pleaded with him'* (Luke 15:25–28).

 Passage for study and prayer: Luke 15:11–32

Although known as the parable of the Prodigal Son, this story told by Jesus might just as well be called the parable of the Two Brothers. The setting of the parable, described in verses 1 and 2, as well as the stories of the lost sheep and lost coin earlier in the chapter, give us the clue. The focus is not so much on the younger brother who repented and returned to his father's house, as on the elder one, who refused to share his father's joy at the prodigal's return. Jesus was aiming to convict the Pharisees and scribes of their false righteousness, spiritual pride and lack of love in their rejection of those who did not keep to their rigid interpretation of the religious rules.

Today, this parable is as relevant as ever – in many contexts, but including that of the Jews and Israel. So many Christians behave just like the older brother. They resent the restoration of the nation and the signs of God's blessing – after all, in their opinion, the Jews rejected Jesus and crucified the Messiah and have been punished for it ever since. The Lord has no right to accept Israel again, to pour out His love and blessing on her, to receive her again into the family, even though she has not as yet corporately acknowledged her Messiah. The older brother is jealous – he has not had a party thrown for him! Yet as the father gently reminds him, he lives continually in his father's house; all the blessings are his already, and the father does not love him any the less. The plea is for him to share his father's joy, to love as his father does and so help to restore the repentant prodigal.

 Prayer Guide

Give thanks that you are adopted into God's family as a beloved child, and pray that you may be delivered from the spirit of the elder brother, in relation to any other of His children, but especially the Jews. *'And he said to him, "Son, you are always with me, and all that I have is yours"'* (v31). Ask the Father for more of His love for your brothers, and ask for opportunities to share that love every day.

Beseech the Lord to forgive and remove the spirit of resentment towards the Jews and Israel found in many Christian circles today, and open Christian eyes to see how much they owe to their Jewish brethren. Pray that God's heart of love for His beloved son (Hosea 11:1–4) will be felt and shared by His Gentile children around the world.

Pray fervently for the 'younger brother' to return to the Father in repentance and be restored fully into fellowship with Him. *'I will arise and go to my father, and will say to him, "Father, I have sinned against heaven and before you, and I am no longer worthy to be called your son"'* (v18).

YOU MUST BE KIDDING!

> *'I say then, has God cast away His people? Certainly not! For I also am an Israelite, of the seed of Abraham, of the tribe of Benjamin. God has not cast away His people whom He foreknew'* (Romans 11:1, 2).

 Passage for study and prayer: Romans 11:1–15

There are many Christians in the world today who consider that God has finished with the Jews. They say that when the Jewish people as a whole rejected Jesus, they forfeited their covenant relationship with God. Since then, the Church has replaced Israel as God's covenant people and all the promises in the Old Testament are now applied to the Church alone. Jews who come to faith in Jesus become Christians and renounce their previous faith. Modern Israel is just a historical anachronism, and has nothing to do with fulfilment of prophecy or God's end-time purposes.

In fact, this doctrine of 'replacement theology' had its roots in the early church. Christians (literally, 'Messianics') were originally a sect within Judaism, but tensions between Jews and Gentile believers grew by the second century into a serious breach between church and synagogue. Mutual rejection and antagonism by religious leaders on both sides led the (Gentile) Early Church Fathers to sever all connections with biblical Judaism. So Sabbath became Sunday, Passover became Easter, etc.

In writing to the Roman believers, however, Paul kills the notion of replacement theology stone dead. His answer to the suggestion is the Greek equivalent of the modern expression, 'You must be kidding!' or 'Don't be ridiculous!' A remnant of Jews has received the revelation of God's grace in Jesus (vv5, 7), but the rest are blinded as the prophets foretold, so that the Gentiles could receive salvation in their place and so provoke them to jealousy (v11). If their temporary stumbling brings such riches to the Gentiles, how much more blessing will come from their eventual restoration (v15)! This is a mystery, but it is all part of God's wonderful plan.

 Prayer Guide

Beseech the Lord to open Christian eyes to the amazing mystery of His plan for Jews and Gentiles in His kingdom. *'I say then, have they stumbled that they should fall? Certainly not! But through their fall, to provoke them to jealousy, salvation has come to the Gentiles'* (v11). Pray for meaningful relationships between Christians and Jews that will reflect the love of Jesus and provoke Jewish people to jealousy.

Pray that Paul's teaching about Israel may be understood and properly taught and that the error of 'replacement theology' would be exposed and refuted wherever it occurs. *'Now if their fall is riches for the world, and their failure riches for the Gentiles, how much more their fullness!'* (v12). Pray particularly for the ancient churches of the Middle East. They are steeped in these doctrines and thus find it difficult to accept the Old Testament and the prophetic references to Israel's restoration.

Praise God that the final spiritual restoration of Israel will bring widespread revival, literally, 'life from the dead'! Pray earnestly for the fulfilment of this promise, and for the growth of the kingdom of God in Israel and the nations. *'For if their being cast away is the reconciling of the world, what will their acceptance be but life from the dead?'* (v15).

ENEMIES FOR OUR SAKE

> *'Concerning the gospel they are enemies for your sake, but concerning the election they are beloved for the sake of the fathers. For the gifts and the calling of God are irrevocable'* (Romans 11:28, 29).

 Passage for study and prayer: Romans 11:16–36

Paul here continues and expands his explanation of the mystery of Israel and the church – namely that both still have their place in God's eternal and perfect plan for mankind. Israel has been temporarily blinded to the truth of the gospel, to enable the Gentiles to enter into God's covenant, until the full number of them has come in. Then she will be saved by her Deliverer, as the Scriptures foretell. Paul's plea to Gentile believers in Jesus, repeated three times in this passage, is not to be arrogant against the Jewish people. He points out in verse 16 that the branches are only holy because the root is holy! Continuing the analogy of the olive tree, which is a common symbol for Israel in the Old Testament, in verses 17–24 he reminds the grafted-in Gentile branches how much they owe to their Jewish heritage. He warns them that they too could be broken off again, if they do not remain grafted in by faith.

As far as God is concerned, the Jews are both enemies (for our sake) and beloved (because of the patriarchs). Indeed, He can never revoke – or call back – the gifts and special calling He has given His covenant people. The future salvation of 'all Israel', even if it is only a remnant, is assured. Their disobedience opened the door to us to receive mercy, so that through our mercy, they may also receive mercy once more (vv30–32). In Greek, the word for 'your'– humeteros – means 'possessed by you' and also 'proceeding from you'. How wonderful that we are both the sign of God's mercy, and His channel of it, to the Jewish people! No wonder Paul ends this chapter with a positive outburst of praise to God for His unfathomable wisdom and ways!

 Prayer Guide

Pray for a rediscovery of true Hebraic roots in the Christian Church, giving Christians a proper understanding both of the Jewish background to the New Testament, and the Hebrew Scriptures used by Jesus and the apostles. Pray for the ministries involved in teaching these truths to be both effective and balanced. *'And if some of the branches were broken off, and you, . . . were grafted in among them, and with them became a partaker of the root and fatness of the olive tree, do not boast . . . remember that you do not support the root, but the root supports you'* (vv17, 18).

Pray that the arrogant spirit of so many Christians against Jewish people will be replaced by a sense of gratitude, and an understanding of God's purposes for Israel. *'For I do not desire, brethren, that you should be ignorant of this mystery, lest you should be wise in your own opinion, that blindness in part has happened to Israel until the fullness of the Gentiles has come in'* (v25).

Give thanks that the day is coming when '. . . *all Israel will be saved, as it is written:'* (v26). Pray earnestly for this, and especially that Christian mercy and love will lead many to find God's forgiveness and salvation already given through the Deliverer. *'For as you were once disobedient to God, yet have now obtained mercy through their disobedience, even so these also have now been disobedient, that through the mercy shown you [Gk. your mercy] they also may obtain mercy'* (vv30, 31).

NO LONGER STRANGERS

> '. . . at that time you were without Christ, being aliens from
> the commonwealth of Israel and strangers from the covenants
> of promise, having no hope and without God in the world'
> (Ephesians 2:12).

 Passage for study and prayer: Ephesians 2:11–22

Paul's marvellous letter to the Ephesians is all about the
church. In these key verses he reminds Gentile believers – that
is, most of us – who we once were and what we now are, 'in
Messiah Jesus'. (Did you know that the word 'Christ' simply
means Messiah? 'Christos' is the Greek translation of the
Hebrew 'Moshiach' – Messiah in English – meaning 'Anointed
One'.) Until Jesus died and rose again, we Gentiles were outside God's covenants. We could only enter the outer courts in
the temple, where the trading went on. We could not offer sacrifices to cover our sin, or be part of temple worship. We were
separated, aliens and foreigners. We were not part of God's
people, could not claim God's promises, and had no hope of
knowing Him.

But now, it's a different story! The blood of Messiah has
brought us near. Jesus' sacrifice for sin bought us both access
to God and reconciliation with men. The dividing wall of the
temple that separated Gentiles from the benefits of God's
covenant has been broken down in Jesus, making us one
people in Him. Together we form the new temple, built on the
foundation of apostolic and prophetic testimony, with Messiah
Himself the chief cornerstone. We are no longer enemies as the
temple laws required, but part of the same family. In fact, we
have together a new identity as One New Mankind, made up
of Jewish and Gentile believers united in Jesus. We have been

re-created, so that we can be a dwelling place of God by the Spirit and a witness to the whole world of true peace and unity, as Isaiah foretold (compare Isaiah 57:19 with Ephesians 2:13). In Israel, the One New Mankind made up of Jews, Arabs and other Gentiles from the nations is proving that peace and reconciliation is possible in the Messiah.

 Prayer Guide

Praise God for the incredible privilege of sharing in the covenants and being part of God's people, able to know Him and show forth His glory to the world! *'. . . you are no longer strangers and foreigners, but fellow citizens with the saints and members of the household of God,'* (v19). Pray that as part of the One New Mankind you may be a testimony to Jews and Gentiles alike of God's grace, mercy and truth.

Rejoice that Jesus has made the way for true reconciliation and pray earnestly for a powerful work of the Holy Spirit to unite Jewish and Arab believers in His love and peace, as a testimony to their divided brethren. *'For He Himself is our peace, who has made both one, and has broken down the middle wall of separation, having abolished in His flesh the enmity,'* (vv14, 15a).

Give thanks that the One New Mankind is growing in size, strength and maturity in Israel, and proving a real witness to God's love and power. *'in whom you also are being built together for a dwelling place of God in the Spirit'* (v22). Ask God to raise up more shepherds after His own heart to lead the various different flocks in Israel's diverse society. Pray earnestly for unity, provision of needed resources and protection in the spiritual battle, especially for those who suffer persecution for their faith.

For further information on issues raised in these studies, or to find out more about the ministry of Christian Friends of Israel, please contact:

CFI Communications
PO Box 2687, Eastbourne, E. Sussex BN22 7LZ
Tel: 01323 410810
Email: info@cfi.org.uk www.cfi.org.uk

Registered charity no. 1051316

List of Biblical Passages Used

Genesis
  12:1–9 16
  15 18
  17:1–22 20
  33:18–35:4 22
  45:1–15 24
Leviticus
  18:19–30 26
Numbers
  23:7–24:9 28
Deuteronomy
  8 30
Joshua
  5:13–6:16 32
Ruth
  1:1–18 34
Nehemiah
  4 36
Psalm
  12 38
  33 40
  94 42
  101 44
  122 14
Isaiah
  14:1, 2 46
  19:16–25 48
  22:1–14 50
  22:15–25 52

  43:1–7 54
  49:14–26 56
  55 58
  58:9–12 60
Jeremiah
  3:6–18 62
  8:15–9:1 64
  16:14–21 66
  32 68
Ezekiel
  11:14–21 70
  22:23–31 72
  36:1–15 74
  36:16–38 76
Daniel
  9:1–22 78
Zechariah
  8:20–23 80
Matthew
  23:29–24:14 82
Luke
  11:1–13 12
  15:11–32 84
Romans
  11:1–15 86
  11:16–36 88
Ephesians
  2:11–22 90

Alphabetical List of Studies

A Call to the South – *Isaiah 43:1–7* — 54
A Fountain of Tears – *Jeremiah 8:15–9:1* — 64
A People Dwelling Alone – *Numbers 23:7–24:9* — 28

Blessings and Curses – *Genesis 12:1–9* — 16

Conditions of his Coming – *Matthew 23:29–24:14* — 82

Drawn or Driven – *Jeremiah 16:14–21* — 66

Enemies For Our Sake – *Romans 11:16–36* — 88

Father of Many Nations – *Genesis 17:1–22* — 20
For Your Name's Sake – *Ezekiel 36:16–38* — 76

God Is in Control – *Psalm 33* — 40
God Sees it All – *Psalm 94* — 42
God's Ways Are not Ours – *Isaiah 55* — 58
Going with God's People – *Zechariah 8:20–23* — 80

Heart Transplant – *Ezekiel 11:14–21* — 70

In and Out of Office – *Isaiah 22:15–25* — 52

Joined with Israel – *Isaiah 14:1, 2* — 46

Mercy and Justice – *Psalm 101* — 44

No Longer Strangers – *Ephesians 2:11–22* — 90

One of Three – *Isaiah 19:16–25* 48

Power to Get Wealth – *Deuteronomy 8* 30
Pray for the Peace of Jerusalem – *Psalm 122* 14

Recognising Joseph – *Genesis 45:1–15* 24
Repairer of the Breach – *Isaiah 58:9–12* 60
Ruth and Orpah – *Ruth 1:1–18* 34

Sacrifice to Molech – *Leviticus 18:19–30* 26
Save the Children – *Isaiah 49:14–26* 56
Shechem – *Genesis 33:18–35:4* 22
Standing in the Gap – *Ezekiel 22:23–31* 72

Teach Us to Pray – *Luke 11:1–13* 12
The Mountains of Israel – *Ezekiel 36:1–15* 74
The Right of Inheritance – *Jeremiah 32* 68
The Sword and the Trowel – *Nehemiah 4* 36
The Throne of the Lord – *Jeremiah 3:6–18* 62
The Two Brothers – *Luke 15:11–32* 84
The Valley of Vision – *Isaiah 22:1–14* 50
Title Deeds – *Genesis 15* 18
Two Kinds of Words – *Psalm 12* 38

Understanding by the Books – *Daniel 9:1–22* 78

Whose Side Is God On? – *Joshua 5:13–6:16* 32

You Must Be Kidding! – *Romans 11:1–15* 86